I0754999

To

____

From

____

Date

____

SOPHA RUSH

unrushed living

EMBRACING SIMPLICITY AND SAVORING LIFE'S MOMENTS

Unrushed Living: Embracing Simplicity and Savoring Life's Moments

First Edition, August 2024

Published by:

21154 Highway 16 East
Siloam Springs, AR 72761
dayspring.com

Written by: Sopha Rush
Content Collaboration by: Trieste Vaillancourt
Cover Design by: Jenna Wilusz

Printed in China
Prime: U1224
ISBN: 979-8-88602-407-4

Contents

Introduction

Hello and welcome,

In the rush of life, it has been easy to set aside dreams and get caught up in the hustle. But as I grow in the Lord, it has become more and more important for me to slow down . . . to breathe . . . to spend time simply remembering that I am a child who belongs in God's embrace, loving Him and allowing Him to lead me in His truth. The practice of slowing down has become a lifestyle. I am learning to savor what is around me and to thank Him for it daily. That is my prayer for you as you read this devotional. May the words and prayers you read here inspire you and pull you closer to His heart. May you find yourself enjoying the unrushed and purposeful pursuit of knowing God.

GRATITUDE

Mornings Are for Saying Thank You

Enter His gates with thanksgiving
and His courts with praise;
give thanks to Him and praise His name.
PSALM 100:4

She rose each morning waiting for the sun. In winter it would take longer, and in the summer she could see the gray hint of it coming through the trees as she stepped into the kitchen. She loved the sunrise because it reminded her that a new day meant new hopes, new mercies, new dreams, and new potential. She waited for the sun, just so she could say "Thank You" for what she had, and for what was to come.

When you wake up each morning, whether it's clear or cloudy, the sun comes up too. The sunrise is a daily reminder of God's nearness. He hasn't forgotten about you or the world you live in, not for a minute. He faithfully brings sunlight and warmth to the day, and moonlight to the night. When you begin the day with "Thank You, God," you're acknowledging the receipt of this gift of fresh new mercies that He's given you. He has already written your story and can't wait to share it with you. Whatever burdened your heart yesterday can be placed safely in His hands as a new day begins. He made this day for you. Go for it.

God,
I come before You with a heart full of gratitude for the precious gift of life. Thank You for each breath, each heartbeat, each second. In every moment, may I recognize the miracle of life that You have given me. I am so grateful that You have chosen me to walk in my purpose alongside You. I pray as I continue to fulfill my purpose, I never take for granted this life.
In Jesus's name, Amen.

GRATITUDE

Thanks at All Times

And whatever you do, whether in word or deed, do it all in the name of the Lord Jesus, giving thanks to God the Father through Him.

COLOSSIANS 3:17

She had decisions to make, every day, in so many ways, that challenged and grew her. She could follow friends. She could listen to experts. But in the end, she knew the answers would come from somewhere deep inside. The best steps forward were the ones she took with God's wisdom in her mind and His truth in her heart. And as she took those steps, she would do so with thanks on her lips. Because no matter what, her goal was to give Him glory.

Every day is best lived with the knowledge that God is at your side. Not only that, but Isaiah 52:12 promises that He goes both before and behind you as well. You're surrounded in the very best way. Whatever you face, there is enough grace for it. People tend to get so worried about things that might happen. But maybe that's because we just haven't gotten there yet. In the middle of whatever decision we're making or circumstance we're facing, when God's presence is there too, there is nothing we can't get through. And *going through* is nothing to be afraid of when we know that God works all things together for the good of those who love Him (Romans 8:28)! *All things*, He says. The good and the hard, the risky and the comfortable. In His care, gratitude always belongs on our lips. Take a moment now to thank Him for something wonderful and something difficult in your life. Even if you can't see how it will all take shape, you can be sure that the shape it's taking is being molded by His loving hands.

God,

You are so gracious and loving. It's Your grace that sustains me and overwhelms my heart with thankfulness. May I always be reassured of Your presence in every single thing that I do. May my life reflect Your love, extending the same grace that You have given to me on a daily basis.

In Jesus's name, Amen.

GRATITUDE

Thanks in All Things

Give thanks in all circumstances;
for this is God's will for you in Christ Jesus.
I THESSALONIANS 5:18

Money was tight, and she couldn't see a way out. But she looked down at the bill-strewn table and remembered all the people who had sat around it. She smiled at the dog under that table, remembering how she had always longed for her own furry friend. "Thank You," she whispered. For the table. For the dog. For the sweet-smelling candle burning on the windowsill and the cell phone by her side, buzzing soon with an invitation to coffee by a friend. It was a good life, after all.

God knows. He knows how you feel and what you need. And He knows you need gratitude. Gratitude is the salve for an aching heart and a starving mind. Gratitude fills empty places that grief or sadness are scrambling to fill. God knows we need to process and mourn at times. But He also understands that in the darkness, gratitude adds the light and warmth that keep hope alive. Instead of focusing on what you lack, spend some time thinking about the abundance that you *do* have. Your home, relationships, or job situation may not be what you'd like, but you have enough for today, don't you? Pray with thanks for the people in your life and the roof over your head. Pray with thanks for a God whose kingdom is at hand in your circumstances. As gratitude floods your thoughts, your circumstances may not have changed, but your outlook will have. And with that, you can get through anything.

God,

You provide in all ways, in all good things. May I always express my gratitude for the abundance that has been generously poured over in my life. Thank You—not just for providing for me spiritually, but for meeting me where I am emotionally and physically. May I always be a good steward of the blessings You have given me and use them to bring You glory.

In Jesus's name, Amen.

GRATITUDE

Through the Valley

Therefore, since we are receiving a kingdom that cannot be shaken, let us be thankful, and so worship God acceptably with reverence and awe.

HEBREWS 12:28

This, *she thought,* is not something I would choose for myself. *In fact, she might rather go in for a root canal or go skydiving from the top of the world's tallest building. But she also knew God. She trusted in His ability to lead her well and in His desire to see her thrive. So she closed her eyes, said thanks to Him, and leapt forward with faith.*

Would you have guessed years ago that things would turn out how they have today? Would you have known that the difficulties would shape you for the stronger? Would you have been brave enough to ask for them, knowing that short-term pain would lead to a version of yourself that could only come by refinement and testing? Most of us would have a difficult time saying yes to it at the beginning of a hard road. But when we can look back and say we would do it all again because of the benefits—of knowing both God and ourselves better—it's easier to see why it was good that we didn't have a clear view of how it all would go. And when we've been through it—*really through it*—saying yes again comes with an extra glimmer of hope and expectation. Think of a season or situation in your life that you would not have chosen. How has it enriched your understanding? How has it blessed your journey? If you don't see the good right now, ask God to show you how things would be different without having lived your story so far. He knows what He's doing. And He will give you so many reasons to be thankful.

God,

it's not always easy walking through hard seasons and facing challenges I don't understand. May I know that through them, I grow and mature into who You are wanting me to become. May Your wisdom always guide me and Your strength sustain me. When I am walking through the valley, may I always keep my eyes fixed on You and not lose sight of my purpose, for You are working all things out for my good. For that, I'm forever grateful.

In Jesus's name, Amen.

GRATITUDE

The Weight of Worth

Give thanks to the LORD, for He is good;
His love endures forever.

I CHRONICLES 16:34

Sometimes the weight of her mistakes and inabilities staggered her. Sometimes her shortcomings stared back at her in the mirror, and it took big work to turn her thoughts around. But she knew what to do. First, she brought to mind a Scripture that was true. Then she told it to herself, reminding her spirit to take heart and her heart to be thankful. After all, she was a child of the King, and He thought the world of His daughter.

Giving thanks isn't always the most natural response to the world around us. And sometimes it feels downright impossible when it's our own selves that drag us down. We are unfortunate champions when it comes to destructive self-talk and the lack of self-confidence. Yet, here we are, card-carrying members of the kingdom of heaven, with pages and pages of promises from God about who we are and what He has called us to be and to do. When we focus on ourselves, we will fail over and over again. We'll constantly see why we *can't*, instead of dwelling on the fact that He *can*. But when we can view our lives through the lens of His love, even our imperfection will feel like a gift worth giving to the One who is molding us into His likeness. What weighs you down today? How are you allowing your inability to control what God is able to do in and with you? Remember your identity in Christ, accept His forgiveness, and then shed that weight of shame. What God has for you is so much better.

God,

thank You for being such an amazing Father who forgives. I know I've made a lot of mistakes and had to learn a lot of lessons along the way, but still my heart is filled with gratitude because of Your love for me. I don't deserve it, I could never earn it, yet You redeem, restore, and renew. May I extend the same forgiveness to myself and others and walk in freedom.

In Jesus's name, Amen.

GRATITUDE

God of Abundance

So then, just as you received Christ Jesus as Lord, continue to live your lives in Him, rooted and built up in Him, strengthened in the faith as you were taught, and overflowing with thankfulness.

COLOSSIANS 2:6–7

She could feel the difference day to day whether or not she had prioritized her time with God. On the days when she was aware of Him, praying, giving thanks, reading the Bible or directing her thoughts toward Him, she felt richer and, fuller. On other days, she felt drained. On those days she wanted to kick herself. Sometimes she did kick. But on wiser days, she just corrected her direction and looked up again, thanking Him for all the goodness He had surrounded her with.

Springtime in itself is a gift. Blossoms on flowering shrubs, bright green leaves bursting from branches, and swelling creeks and riverbeds brimming with the evidence of all that has been brewing beneath the cool surfaces of winter. Depending on where you live, the abundance may look different. But even those who live in a climate where it is more warm than cold—or more cold than hot—we all know what spring looks like. And in Christ, we know what it feels like. After all, we can't plug ourselves into the Source of all things creative and lovely and life-giving and not experience that fullness ourselves. Life in Jesus brings joy even in darker winter seasons. His hope is always coursing through us. And no matter where we look, we will see His beauty, brought forth for our benefit, all around. Where can you see and feel His abundance in your life today?

God,

thank You for surrounding me with Your beauty every day. I am in awe of the details that You have put in everything You do. You do everything with such excellence, and I pray that I may be a good steward of appreciating what You have given me. May I always find the beauty in slowing down and being grateful for what's around me, and what's in front of me.

In Jesus's name, Amen.

GRATITUDE

Open Doors

Always giving thanks to God the Father for everything, in the name of our Lord Jesus Christ.

EPHESIANS 5:20

She wouldn't have written it this way if she'd had the pen . . . and for that, she was constantly thankful. God's ideas far outshined her own. He gave her the desires that filled her heart, and then He went above and beyond with things she never could have dreamed of. This story of hers was getting more and more beautiful. Not because it was all perfect, but because of God. He filled the gaps, wrote it all down, and gave her reasons to be thankful every single day.

God never said we had to make our own way. Work hard, yes. Dream big, yes. Pursue excellence, even—that is a yes. But our biggest goals in Jesus are so *not stressful*. He asks that we delight ourselves in Him (Psalm 37:4), believe in Him (Romans 10:9), and know that He is God (Psalm 46:10). When we direct our efforts toward placing all of our hope in Him, it opens the door for Him to do His most amazing, complete, exciting, over-the-top work in our lives. It gives

Him room to shape our own hearts' desires into the treasures He longs to give. He takes everything broken and makes it new. And He sets paths before us that we never would have reached if it weren't for His tender mercies. Where are you in your journey of surrender and rest in the Lord? If you're holding on to anything today, don't be afraid to leave it in His hands.

God,

You are the Father of limitless possibilities. I am so grateful for the opportunities You continue to place before me. You have given me the chance to learn, grow, and be pruned in every single season. May I have the wisdom to discern what opportunities are from You and only You. May You go before me and close doors that need to be shut and open ones that are just for me.

In Jesus's name, Amen.

GRATITUDE

Weapons of Hope

Do not be anxious about anything, but in every situation, by prayer and petition, with thanksgiving, present your requests to God. And the peace of God, which transcends all understanding, will guard your hearts and your minds in Christ Jesus.

PHILIPPIANS 4:6–7

She hid herself in God. From here she could see the swirls of uncertainty in her situation. But from in here, where it was warm and safe and so full of peace, she knew it was all going to work out. It would not be easy, but she would move through it with a buoyancy that only trusting God could bring. And somehow, getting through difficult times in this way would make her stronger . . . more courageous . . . more complete.

It doesn't have to make sense to be beautiful. When we go through life with the expectation that everything is going to be smooth and simple and easy, we will be let down again and again. But when we expect the things that God promises, the things that Jesus is, then peace and joy are always available. It can take some real focus. It can take blind faith. It can take a very mindful deep breath and a reminder to yourself that God is the Master of all the universe. But you have prayer—a weapon of possibility. You have a Father who wants to hear what you have to say. You have a voice with which you can say "Thank You" over and over to the One who fills and blesses your days. As you rely on these tools, the peace that passes understanding will guard your heart and mind.

God,

I am truly thankful for this peace You have given me. Even in the midst of uncertainty, I know that the peace I have surpasses all understanding. Yes, life can be hard, it can be painful at times, yet Your peace covers and guards my heart. I am so grateful for such moments of reassurance knowing that You are here with me all along, never leaving me, always protecting me.

In Jesus's name, Amen.

GRATITUDE

This Is the Day

The Lord is my strength and my shield;
my heart trusts in Him, and He helps me.
My heart leaps for joy,
and with my song I praise Him.
PSALM 28:7

Every day when she opened her eyes, no matter what she was facing, she knew she could do it with joy. She had God on her side, after all. And with God she had history. Good history, where He had shown up and demonstrated His faithfulness to her in all sorts of ways. She reminded herself as often as she could that putting her trust in God would always take her to the very best places.

Every morning is a renewed promise from God that your life has value and purpose. Yesterday might not have turned out how you'd planned. Today you might be facing fears, challenges, and expectations that have you on edge. But today hasn't happened yet, first thing in the morning, and there's no way to determine what course your life will take over the next twenty-four hours. More importantly, there's no way of knowing how God plans on showing up. Fear is a package from the enemy that you can refuse to sign for. Or if you find anxious thoughts inside you already, stamp a big *CANCELLED BY HOPE* across them and send them back where they belong. You are a champion already, not because of what you've accomplished today, but because of the good work God is accomplishing in and through you. "This is the day the LORD has made" (Psalm 118:24 NKJV), and He made it just for you.

God,
may I fall on my knees in Your presence every morning that I wake. I want to pursue You and let my heart be shaped by Your truth before distractions try to cloud my space. May You give me a clear mind and a fresh new start to glorify You. I don't ever want to lose my praise for You. I want my heart to be filled with gratitude, knowing that Your presence is a gift.
In Jesus's name, Amen.

GRATITUDE

Attitude Matters

For God has not given us a spirit of fear and timidity, but of power, love, and self-discipline.

II TIMOTHY 1:7 NLT

She was learning, over the years, that God's gifts were free and forever. Sometimes she had to remind herself that they were available. But when she did, she always felt stronger and more ready to face the things before her. God had given her life a big "Yes" the moment she had said yes to Him. That was a powerful thought. She was loved beyond measure. And she had everything she needed to thrive each day. Knowing all of this made her so very thankful.

One of the most powerful tools we can use is the ability to say thanks. We can thank our spouse. We can thank our kids. We can thank the person who brings the mail. And of course, every day, in a million ways, we can thank God. Gratitude brings an instant attitude adjustment. Whatever darkens our thoughts can't stand to be given the light of joy and thankfulness. It's not that the trouble goes away. But with gratitude, we begin to see that things are rarely as bleak and difficult as they seem when the lights are off. Even the most hopeless-looking situations seem to lighten in the knowledge of the Helper, the Holy Spirit, surrounding us with love and comfort. Where could your attitude use an adjustment today? In which areas of your life are you feeling a sense of hopelessness? Find the things you can thank God for. Keep a list. It will make a difference.

God,

may I learn the importance of counting my blessings. Each day I want to wake up with gratitude, thankful to see another day. May I not let the worries of yesterday carry over into this new day. May joy overwhelm my spirit and worry be replaced with thanksgiving. There's so much around me to be grateful for. Open my eyes, Lord, to see what You see, to hear what You hear.

In Jesus's name, Amen.

GRATITUDE

The way we deal with uncertainty says a lot about whether Jesus is ahead of us leading, or behind us just carrying our stuff.

—BOB GOFF

SIMPLICITY

Living without Distraction

But godliness with contentment is great gain. For we brought nothing into the world, and we can take nothing out of it.

I TIMOTHY 6:6–7

She found herself caring more about what was on her newsfeed than who or what was in the room where she sat. Instead of silhouettes and the soft breathing of her loved ones, she fell asleep with the images on the screen still burning behind her eyelids. So one day she found courage. She turned it all off. She embraced the holiness of the everyday, decluttered her brain and heart, and chose to tune in to the people and pleasures in her immediate world.

Simplicity is one of the most underrated virtues. We get so caught up in how much we can own and how fancy we can look to everyone else. But somewhere deep inside, we know that the message of Jesus is a simple truth and that we simply have to live like we believe it. He tells us to come to Him like little children. And one of the things that children do very well is live in the present. They can make moments with a peanut butter sandwich or a wooden train set feel like the most unwasted, precious times. Children laugh with abandon, cry with passion, snuggle with complete trust, and fall asleep without a care in the world. How would your life be different if you were to start living like a child? What if you didn't let self-awareness get in the way of a giant laugh that fills a crowded restaurant? What if you set aside every distraction just to be on the floor with your children or animals or a good book or crochet pattern? You won't get back the hours you've been given today . . . but you can make these hours some of the sweetest memories of simply living.

God,
there's so much beauty in the simple moments that I find myself taking for granted. May You help me to embrace the joy and peace in the ordinary, to embrace simplicity in every way and focus on what truly matters. May I learn to let go of unnecessary distractions and allow my heart to appreciate what's around me.
In Jesus's name, Amen.

SIMPLICITY

Finding Fulfillment

My God shall supply all your need according to His riches in glory by Christ Jesus.

PHILIPPIANS 4:19 NKJV

Someone had introduced her to that television show where joy was the reason to keep something, and the lack of joy suggested that you give it away. It was work. But little by little, her home was becoming a place of peace. It was shocking how little she really needed to be content. And just as shocking to realize how the clutter had added to her angst. Joy was at her fingertips, and as she prayed each day, God was giving her the heart to love it that way.

Whoever told us that fulfillment comes in boxes off a delivery truck? Where did we get the idea that "add to cart" was the best way to get a burst of dopamine and a sense of peace? Certainly not from God, the One who has absolutely everything and only wants one thing: our hearts. The Source of every treasure wants us to find all of our contentment in Him. Yes, everything was made for our enjoyment (I Timothy 6:17). But we were the ones made for His pleasure (Revelation 4:11 KJV)—and if we are His greatest joy, then He is definitely ours! Spend some time considering what surrounds you in your home and life. Does it add to your true fulfillment, or distract you from it? Does it make you thankful that God is in your life, or is it a tool to keep your mind and senses occupied on other things? There's no shame in making the choice to keep or get rid of something. God knows your heart, and He is helping you align perfectly with the beautiful, contented human He designed you to be.

God,
I want to pray for a simple heart. A heart that seeks contentment in simplicity. May You teach me how to value having a humble spirit and appreciate the beauty of less rather than always wanting more. Remove the desire for unnecessary things in my life and begin to replace it with a spirit of gratefulness. May every blessing that comes my way keep me humble.
In Jesus's name, Amen.

SIMPLICITY

Wonder

And He said: "Truly I tell you, unless you change and become like little children, you will never enter the kingdom of heaven."

MATTHEW 18:3

She watched her children with awe sometimes. They could be amazed by the simplest things, like a bug on a leaf or the exhilaration of leaping off the pool deck into her upstretched, waiting arms. They didn't spend time worrying about tomorrow or even what was for dinner. They didn't know how much love and energy she poured into making sure they could live fearlessly. And that in itself was a lesson for her: God, You do that for me.

Somewhere around middle school, a child's sense of wonder turns inward and morphs into self-awareness. This isn't inherently bad. God doesn't make mistakes. Self-awareness, as it matures, allows us to be mindful about our choices and behaviors. But when it replaces our wonder entirely, that is a problem. Wonder looks at the world through simple and faith-filled eyes. It watches the way the breeze ruffles the grasses along a lake. It dreams of becoming an astronaut. Wonder opens the world as wide as it can be and sparks gratitude for God's incredible creativity. Wonder slows us down and turns our focus toward the way God sees us instead of the way the world does. It takes a child's wonder to believe that all God says is true. Children will dance when they're happy, seek comforting arms when they're sad, and color a page with bold strokes. They aren't yet tempered by fear of failure or foolishness. Today, open your heart to the possibilities that childlike faith will offer.

God,
thank You for giving me a childlike faith. I pray for a simple faith that allows me to walk closely to You daily. May I always be willing to learn and my faith in You be made pure and rooted in Your love. May I continue to have eyes that see what Your heart desires.
In Jesus's name, Amen.

SIMPLICITY

How You See It

Set your minds on things above, not on earthly things.
COLOSSIANS 3:2

When she saw that it was raining outside, her first reaction was disappointment. This meant boots and an umbrella, when today she was in the mood for sandals and sunglasses. Then she checked her heart. There would be days for sunshine, but rainy days could be fun too. In fact, she kicked off her boots as she stepped outside. She grabbed a jacket with a cozy hood and went out to dance barefooted in the puddles.

Like raindrops on your skin, the blessings of God are simply everywhere . You don't need to work for them (though hard work will often bring them). You don't need to ask for them (though He loves to answer your prayers). Knowing God means you're always in view of the beauty He infuses into every living moment. Right where you are, right now, stop for a moment and look around. What do you see? Where is His goodness? Is it in the warmth of your coffee? The purr of a cat? The color of your socks? The person in the next room? The glint of the sun off the vase on the table? It doesn't take a simple mind, but a simple choice to filter out the noise and settle your heart and mind on one . . . little . . . blessing. Every time you do, you invite peace to fill your soul. When it rains, either enjoy the fact that the flowers are getting a drink or go and dance in the puddles. Choosing to celebrate the moment will feed you so much more than wishing away the clouds.

God,

thank You for the simple blessings that You shower me with every day. May my heart always remain in a posture that is full of gratitude, appreciating the beauty of ordinary moments around me. May there be joy and peace that comes with recognizing Your presence in the quiet moments of my life. Even in the simplest blessings, I am reminded of Your goodness that overflows.

In Jesus's name, Amen.

SIMPLICITY

In His Hands

When anxiety was great within me,
your consolation brought me joy.
PSALM 94:19

It took a minute to realize she'd been holding her breath. Every muscle felt tight like springs ready to pop. The conversation hadn't gone well. Now the tears came as she worried what this meant for the relationship. Releasing her breath, she managed a weak, "Oh, Jesus." And something shifted. She breathed again, deeply. "Jesus." He seemed to respond in a wave of love, softening her tense muscles and filling her with a hope that didn't currently make sense. I have you both, *He seemed to say.* Don't give up just yet.

Women were made for heavy burdens. We carry so much, whether it's through friendship or motherhood, schooling or careers, marriage or ministry, or all of the above. We would break if we could, except that the weight of responsibility prevents us from dropping a single thing without our consent. Oh, we drop things. We lose it. We beg for mercy when we need to. But the simplest answer is the quietest whisper that resonates the loudest in our hearts: "Jesus." He invites us to leave everything in His hands and take up the yoke that is lighter and easier than anything we would carry on our own (Matthew 11:28–30). He's been there, after all. He's experienced everything. He knows what we need, and He knows we need Him more than we need to breathe. Jesus carries us even as He carries what worries us. In Him, a woman can have it all while holding on to nothing.

God,
there is beauty in being able to surrender
my worries and fears to You. May I learn to trust
in Your plan and find simplicity in surrender.
I know it's not always easy letting go of the
burdens that I have had to carry, but I know You
have come alongside me so I don't have to carry
the weight on my own. Once I am released, I pray
for Your peace, knowing You are in control.
In Jesus's name, Amen.

SIMPLICITY

Simple Faith

Your faithfulness continues through all generations; You established the earth, and it endures.

PSALM 119:90

She was taking a risk. As long as she didn't think about it too much, she knew she could do it. But when her mind wandered, the fear started to creep in. Who did she think she was, anyway? Eventually her mind quieted. The whisper of peace found its way into her heart. And she remembered that she was made just for this. God was within her. And with Him, she could not fail.

There will be voices inside your head and all around you, telling you that you're not good enough. You'll want to believe them. The evidence will stack up, proving that there's no way you can make a difference big enough to matter to God or anyone else. There will be those voices everywhere. You'll never have to search for a reason not to be brave. But listen more closely, and you'll hear another sound. Gentler, more confident, less urgent—*I am with you* (Isaiah 41:10).

The world produces confusion and doubt. But walking with God brings a calm to any storm and hope to any challenge. Even when you move into territory you've never experienced before, you can be sure that God is two steps ahead (Deuteronomy 31:8). He knows what He's doing. He knows who you are. Your steps can be sure as you trust Him and lean into His promises. What new thing are you facing today? Breathe a prayer, then step forward with simple faith. You won't be going alone.

God,
thank You for being a faithful Father. You have set me on a path where I know wholeheartedly that no matter what, You go before me. May You remove any doubts or unnecessary fears from this journey marked by simplicity. I want to trust in Your promises and walk with a simple, unwavering faith. I want my heart to be forever anchored to You.
In Jesus's name, Amen.

SIMPLICITY

Priorities

"But seek first His kingdom and His righteousness, and all these things will be given to you as well."

MATTHEW 6:33

She emptied her mind like she emptied the cluttered hall closet: one thing at a time. She took each thought, mulled on it for a brief time, then put it where it belonged, either away for the moment or away for good. Then she closed her eyes and focused on the promises she knew by heart: God, You are so good. You hold me in the palm of Your hand. You hold all things together. Today I am held and full of hope. *With a clear mind and a sure faith, she began her day simply feeling loved.*

God doesn't mind when we want things. He designed us with likes and dislikes. Some of us are collectors of objects and others of us collect travels. Some of us fill our homes with pets, and others of us DIY our home décor. We might be urban foodies or rural farmers, but along with our lifestyles come big dreams. God often delights in providing for those dreams. What matters most, though, is what matters most to us. Do you let the lives of influencers and friends dictate your mood based on how you think you measure up to their picture-perfect posts? Do you prefer certain brands just because they're popular or because you value quality? Does the *you* in you take precedence over the *God* in you? The promise of Matthew 6:33 is that when we turn our attention and priority toward the things of God and His Kingdom, we won't lack for any good thing. That doesn't mean that if we "pray right" we can expect our dream yacht to be overnighted to the front door. But it does mean that God will help us to arrange our priorities in such a way that all of His good plans for us will come to be. Contentment comes by simply gazing at Jesus.

God,
there are so many things in this world that want to distract me from what You have going for me. I pray for a mind that is clear from the clutter and distractions. May I begin to focus and discern what really matters and embrace thoughts that reflect Your wisdom and character. May my mind be a continual dwelling place of Your peace and simplicity.
In Jesus's name, Amen.

SIMPLICITY

Contentment

*I am not saying this because I am in need,
for I have learned to be content
whatever the circumstances.
I know what it is to be in need,
and I know what it is to have plenty.
I have learned the secret of being content
in any and every situation, whether well fed
or hungry, whether living in plenty or in want.*
PHILIPPIANS 4:11–12

She had more now than she did then. Most of the time it was wonderful, and she was thankful. But sometimes she could tell that she was forgetting what it was like to be in need. In a way, having less kept her dependent on God. Abundance made her work to remember that everything she owned was a gift that could go away tomorrow. So she made a point of finding contentment not in things, but in the Giver of every good gift (James 1:17). That way, she would always find her joy.

What would happen to your attitude if you lost everything tomorrow? Could you recover? If your most prized possessions went up in flames, could you bounce back? It might not feel possible right now, but if you've hidden yourself in Jesus, then His grace would be there. What if tomorrow you woke up in the apartment you had in college or with your first job? Would you be equally as thankful now as you were then? Contentment sometimes feels like the elusive unicorn of life. We want what we used to have, or what we don't have yet, instead of the incredible mercy and provision we have today. Contentment creates even ground, no matter your situation. It makes it possible to be neutral about driving a new car or the one you've had for a few years. Contentment gives you as much gratitude for a bowl of soup as it does for a giant burger. Contentment makes God the star of the story. Everything else is just cake.

God,
thank You for being a provider who never lacks. You go before me daily and give me a peace that covers me. May I receive the gift of contentment and live a life of simplicity. May I find joy in the present moment and stop trying to rush to what's ahead. I don't want to miss out on what You are doing now in my pursuit of wanting more. May I rest in Your abundance of love.
In Jesus's name, Amen.

SIMPLICITY

The Good Life

Then He said to them,
"Watch out! Be on your guard against
all kinds of greed;
life does not consist in
an abundance of possessions."
LUKE 12:15

She found herself smiling more often now. There was time for it. In the past, the drive for more and better would often wear her to the bone, sending her straight to bed in the evenings, only to find her before sunup each morning to wear her out all over again. But now . . . oh, now, she had found balance. Or at least she had tasted it. She worked, yes. But her days were driven by love and pleasure now. Becoming a child of God had shifted her priorities. She always had enough, and that included laughter and peace and a home that thrived in Jesus.

What does it benefit us to chase after the things that God wants to give us in His own time? It's not that He says no to things like vacations or new cars. It's that He wants us to be hidden in Him first, knowing and trusting that the good life will always be best when He is the priority. Left alone, people tend to life like revving race cars. We burn gas faster than we can make money to buy more. The good life in God is much more like a thrilling roller coaster. Buckled in and safe, we ride the rails with our hand in His, trusting that every twist and turn will take us to the destination He's designed. Consider today where you want to be tomorrow. Are you chasing the right things? The right person? Are you trusting His timing and His process, or do you need to take your foot off the gas and get out of the fast lane? It's never too late to adjust priorities and find a healthy balance.

God,
there's a richness in simplicity. Teach me to appreciate the beauty all around me. May I not let the world define what rich looks like for me, but instead, let me be reassured that my riches are found in You, for You have made me rich in Your love, peace, and grace. May my life reflect just that.
In Jesus's name, Amen.

SIMPLICITY

Becoming

He who was seated on the throne said,
"I am making everything new!"
Then He said, "Write this down,
for these words are trustworthy and true."
REVELATION 21:5

Looking back through her journal, she was amazed. The things on her mind just a few years or months ago had almost all been addressed by God by now. She had answers, she'd seen plans unfold, there had been closed doors and open ones. Some things had worked out so differently than she'd hoped—some for the better and some more difficult. But she knew from experience that even the tough times were just waiting rooms for God's goodness to shine through. He was always doing something new.

A caterpillar never fights back. The instinct is deep inside to eat and eat, finally submitting to a chrysalis and allowing its entire body to break down. It's doubtful that it hears from other butterflies before submitting to the process. It just knows its job. It's doubtful, too, that the hungry little caterpillar could ever have guessed at the beautiful, free feeling of flitting on the breeze with brightly colored wings.

The whole life of a caterpillar is about becoming. And while the DNA of a butterfly is exactly the same as the crawling creature it was before, almost nothing else is recognizable. We are constantly becoming too. Our DNA never changes because we are always the children God created us to be, but He never stops molding us into His likeness. Unlike a caterpillar, we do fight back when we think we know better. But letting Him work releases us into the constant newness of life in Him.

God,

thank You for making all things new. There's so much truth in knowing that no matter what is going on in my life, I know that You are working and creating a space for me to grow and appreciate the simplicity of change. May I be willing to let go so I can make room for what You are going to do through me. I want to be open to receive the goodness that flows from You.

In Jesus's name, Amen.

SIMPLICITY

Joy comes to us
in ordinary moments.
We risk missing out
when we get too busy
chasing down
the extraordinary.

—BRENÉ BROWN

REST

A Part of the Plan

Return to your rest, my soul,
for the Lord has been good to you.
PSALM 116:7

When her heart got busy, the tug became real. It was an invitation she felt deep inside to convalesce. Not that she was overly broken. But she was beginning to recognize, as she got older, that life tended to wear her down but that God would build her up again. Over and over, she would return to the cocoon of His love and find herself restored, renewed, and stronger than before.

Nothing will come of the past now—what's done is done. There are no promises for the future yet. But today . . . oh, today. The richness of this moment when you get to breathe air, feel the sun, watch kids play, feel sorrow and strong hugs, make plans, and see how God's plans have unfolded. Somewhere along the way we've learned that the hustle is everything. If we're not working toward tomorrow, then are we really accomplishing anything of value? But when we live that way, we're forgetting that God is at work. We also forget that rest is a part of the plan. For some reason, it's become an act of courage to choose rest over other things, but for God, He asks it of us. *Slow down,* He says. *Look around you. Remember where you've been and take a look at where you are. Daydream about tomorrow.* When was the last time you truly rested? When did you sit on the back porch and sip a cup of tea? When did you lie in bed for thirty minutes before turning to your phone? When did you choose to trust God that resting is a part of your wiring? Make time today to rest. You'll find Him waiting there for you.

God,
thank You for the gift of being able to rest. There's beauty in being able to reflect on the goodness of what You are doing in my life. May I slow down long enough to draw near to You always. I want my heart to be filled with thanksgiving and gratitude without my thoughts always rushing to the next thing.
In Jesus's name, Amen.

REST

Rest Stops

Yes, my soul, find rest in God;
my hope comes from Him.
Truly He is my rock and my salvation;
He is my fortress, I will not be shaken.
My salvation and my honor depend on God;
He is my mighty rock, my refuge.
Trust in Him at all times, you people;
pour out your hearts to Him,
for God is our refuge.

PSALM 62:5–8

Sometimes she forgot to slow down. When she remembered, she wondered why she forgot so often! Her body needed the respite from constantly moving forward. Her mind needed to dwell on God and His goodness. Her soul needed encouragement. After these little breaks, she always felt energized and more aware of God's presence.

The best hikes are long ones with a beautiful view at the end. And the best backpacks to have on good hikes are filled with trail mix and water or whatever snack you prefer. Choose your own adventure. But any uphill climb will involve stopping points, a place where you find a flat rock or tree stump to sit on and be refreshed. On the right day, you'll see squirrels, chipmunks, marmots, or birds watching you curiously to see if you'll drop a peanut from your hand. If you're near water, you'll hear the sound of it bubbling along, and if it's breezy, you'll hear the branches rustle up high. You'll hear your own breathing as you rest from the effort for a minute or two. You'll notice the smell of pines or firs, the wet ground after it wakes up from winter. Pausing to rest doesn't detract from the hiking experience; in fact, it will probably make it richer. Whatever climb you face today, remember to rest in the middle of it. Find God, your Rock, and sit with Him awhile. When you stand again to move forward, you will be even more ready for what's to come.

God,

thank You for renewing my mind and spirit. You have given me such strength to overcome any obstacle that has come my way. Though it hasn't been easy, I know that with You by my side, You continue to keep my mind sharp. I can rest knowing that I don't have to do anything alone. I know You are with me every step of the way, and I cling to that truth.

In Jesus's name, Amen.

REST

First and Foremost

"So do not fear, for I am with you;
do not be dismayed, for I am your God.
I will strengthen you and help you;
I will uphold you with My righteous right hand."
ISAIAH 41:10

Alcohol. Gaming. Shopping. Spilling the tea about other people's problems. She and her friends had experienced every kind of distraction. If she didn't have firsthand experience, she'd seen it in the ones she loved. And there was entertainment, yes. But there was never fulfillment. There was only wanting more of what wasn't satisfying. Finally one day she decided to tell God she was sorry and to start again. He helped her to choose wisely and set limits. It was then that her whole life began to sing.

What we don't often consider is how the things we seek for entertainment take a toll on our bodies. Literally anything that becomes our center of focus begins to eat away at our happiness and effectiveness for God. Exercising is wonderful, but it can become a god. Scrolling can be all-consuming.

The work of making and spending money can actually become more expensive to our joy than living simply and frugally. God has provided everything for our enjoyment, but He gives us the responsibility of learning what is good for us and setting the right limits. If we're not setting our minds on Christ, then what exactly are we aiming for? What about you? Are you seeking your rest in Jesus, or are you mistaking entertainment for rest? Ask Him to clear your mind and help you find your peace in Him first and foremost. From there, everything else will fall into place. And you just might find that the things you once turned to were actually keeping you from peace in the first place.

God,
may I find rest in You and only You. I pray You fill my heart with Your peace that continues to surpass all understanding. May I trust You like never before and rest assured that You have everything figured out. I don't have to wear these burdens anymore. I know that Your peace is sufficient for what I need, and that alone is good enough for me.
In Jesus's name, Amen.

REST

Sharing the Load

"Come to Me, all you who are weary and burdened, and I will give you rest. Take My yoke upon you and learn from Me, for I am gentle and humble in heart, and you will find rest for your souls. For My yoke is easy and My burden is light."

MATTHEW 11:28–30

"God, take this please." It had become her cry for whenever a burden was too heavy. With her kids, her husband, her friends, her finances, her mental or physical health, she knew it wasn't a weight for her alone to bear. She spoke the name of Jesus over anything that troubled her. It didn't make the circumstances easier, but she was less soul-weary. And releasing it all to Him gave her space to gaze on His beauty as He worked in ways that only He can.

Allowing God to help us does many things for us. First, the burden of it all is lifted when we start to acknowledge His incredible power and love. Just knowing that Someone capable is on our side makes a big difference. Hearing other people's stories about

God's faithfulness can strengthen our resolve to move forward in hope. And since we really can't do it all ourselves anyway, it puts our hearts in the right place. You are not meant to be a lone soldier. Maybe life has gone that way for you. Maybe you've had to handle it yourself. Maybe you've learned through family or circumstances that there's no one else you can count on. If that's you . . . I'm so sorry. If there's a blessing in it, it's knowing that we're not supposed to place our trust in anyone but God. When no one else comes through, it forces our perspective. We can choose to protect our hearts alone or believe that God will take the burden. Can you trust Him?

God,

my heart longs to worship You. To rest in Your presence. I'm tired, but I know that with an open heart, You restore what has been taken from me. You replenish my spirit with joy and give me rest that allows me to release the power to control things I cannot and leave them up to You.

In Jesus's name, Amen.

REST

Light in a Dark Place

But those who hope in the Lord will renew their strength. They will soar on wings like eagles; they will run and not grow weary, they will walk and not be faint.

ISAIAH 40:31

So many voices demanded her attention. There were so many needs around her that she wasn't even sure what her own were at the moment. Did she need quiet? Conversation? A glass of water or a nap? She was confused. So, right where she was, she closed her eyes and prayed. Find me, Jesus. *She allowed everything else to dim so that she could home in on the sound of His voice.* I'VE GOT YOU. *Knowing it deep in her spirit gave her the clarity she needed to jump back into the fray.*

Hope is the superfood of faith. The amount you have never quite lines up with the enormous effect it has on your heart and soul. Like a candle in a cave, one spark of hope will give light to everything around you. Where the darkness held you paralyzed in place, hope brings purpose. But you've got to settle. To stay in that place of confidence, it's important to give God all the room He needs to work. If He's trying to light your way, all your breathless and worried talking is likely to blow that candle out. He doesn't need help, really. He just needs a surrendered, quiet, listening, trusting heart. It's essential to make time and space for that every single day. When God gets your first fruits of availability, you will benefit from all His hope and strength.

God,
may my heart always be open to go deeper with You. I know the world is loud around me, and distractions want to take me away from You. I pray that as I draw near to You, I can rest in knowing there is an abundance of spiritual strength that comes from You. May I stay focused on what's ahead of me and not what's behind.
In Jesus's name, Amen.

REST

When the Storm Comes

Do not be anxious about anything, but in every situation, by prayer and petition, with thanksgiving, present your requests to God. And the peace of God, which transcends all understanding, will guard your hearts and your minds in Christ Jesus.

PHILIPPIANS 4:6–7

She was a girl of action. If something needed to get done, she could do it. She wanted to, especially if it meant things would move forward more quickly or efficiently. It took her a long time to realize that to God, prayer *was an action word.* Thanking, asking, repenting, *and* listening *were all verbs that would lead to peace in God. So she switched her perspective. She gave up on worrying, and often on doing, before praying. That way she knew her actions would hit the mark every time.*

Life is full of storms. That's not a mistake on God's part. But it can be very uncomfortable at times. Though it's hard for us to believe sometimes, the storms we go through will help us to understand

God better if we're open to it. The difference between knowing and not knowing God is what surrounds us through the journey. Would you rather be treading water in the middle of the sea, wondering if anyone is out there looking for you? Or would you rather have a sturdy little boat full of provisions and a two-way radio? Your boat might not fully protect you from the wind and waves. But it will certainly give you a fighting chance, with the knowledge that the Owner of that boat equipped it with GPS before you set out. The waves seem less dangerous when you're warm and buoyant.

God,
whatever my circumstances or the storms I am facing, I know You quiet the waves to a whisper. May I focus on resting in You and not the chaos around me. I know that You are good and faithful and always covering me with Your protection. May I continue to lean into You and not lose sight of the promises that You have set before me.
In Jesus's name, Amen.

REST

The Beauty of Weakness

And God is able to bless you abundantly, so that in all things at all times, having all that you need, you will abound in every good work.
II CORINTHIANS 9:8

How had she fallen into this trap again? She was holding tight on to something she knew she ultimately couldn't control. Yet she knew Someone who could. And He wanted to! She sighed a sorry *to God and mindfully released her grip on the situation.* You are able, *she reminded herself to Him. And guess what? He was. And He did. And then she did, and it was the best feeling in the world.*

It can be such a strange feeling, trying to balance the fact that we are strong and capable women with the fact that we're welcomed as weak and needy children before God. How can we do both? It has less to do with being one or the other and more to do with the order in which we accept our identity in Christ. Second Corinthians 12:9–11 (and the sweet song "Jesus Loves Me") says that our weakness is what gives His strength the room it needs to work. Like a light bulb plugged into a power source, we can shine as brightly as we were made to. But a light bulb boxed up in a closet is utterly useless. Trying to shine apart from the power source would do nothing. But connecting to God will allow you to operate at your fullest potential. How are you at recognizing the beauty of your own weakness? Is there any area of your life or personality that you want to surrender to His strength today?

God,
it's not always easy letting go. Yet, somehow, I trust that everything is going to work out for my good. It's Your truth that I cling to. At times when I am weak, I rest in knowing You are restoring my spirit and filling me up with Your strength, calming my anxious thoughts and dissolving my worries. I trust in You.
In Jesus's name, Amen.

REST

The Gifts of Life

Every good and perfect gift is from above, coming down from the Father of the heavenly lights, who does not change like shifting shadows.

JAMES 1:17

"It's going to be a good day," she declared to no one as she stepped out the front door. She had no idea what was coming or whom she'd see or talk to. There were no guarantees. But she knew her God was good. She had every reason to expect His presence would be with her all day long. He was a God of good surprises, after all. Even the tough things on her plate were manageable and not absent of joy. With God on her side, this day couldn't fail.

"Today is a gift." You'll find that posted in your feed or spoken by someone you know, but do you know the depth of its truth? Someone considered you and decided that you had value. You were given everything, from the hairs on your head to the breath in your lungs to the nails on your toes. The sun shines for you. The flowers grow. The wave from your neighbor, the emotion that flows when you watch a good movie, the taste of a delicious, iced chai on a hot day—all of it has been orchestrated for your joy. Even the way God shows up in your pain. That is a gift. The comfort you have to offer a hurting child or a friend—that is a gift. None of it has been payment for your striving. What have you taken for granted? Think with gratitude on the things that make your life rich. The more you recognize it and thank God, the more He gives.

God,

help me to slow down when everything around me seems to be going at such a fast pace. I don't want to miss out on what You have for me, always ready for the next thing, seeking what's to come rather than resting in the knowledge that my life isn't a race but a journey to walk alongside You. May I always be reminded to rest in You and not the future.

In Jesus's name, Amen.

REST

Hope for the Broken Places

The Lord replied, "My Presence will go with you, and I will give you rest."
EXODUS 33:14

She had held on so tightly for so long that her fingers were numb. It took years for the gentle invitation of God's willingness to woo her into releasing that grip. His encouragement made her brave, and she remembered that feeling. Indeed, it took all the bravery she could muster to let Him see her softest spots. But there was no judgment. There were no harsh words. There was just love, the tenderest of touches where she most needed to be noticed. He was a patient Healer, and when the time was right, she was whole again.

We bring a lot with us from childhood. Hopefully most of it is wonderful, and you have many reasons to be thankful. But chances are, there are broken things, too, that God is actively healing. It takes time. And in the process we have to learn again to rest. Broken trust usually leads us to protect our vulnerable spots with ferocity instead of submitting them immediately to the Healer. But maturity and time allow us to see how gently He holds us, broken and afraid. It gets easier to run to Him instead of away into hiding. When we finally do believe Him, there's no match for the feeling of letting every muscle relax and every tense spot be ministered to by His love. Where are your most broken places? Are you aware of them, and can you find the bravery to open up to God today? Or are they healed now, marked by a story that you can share with others who deal with pain? No ache is left untouched by His hand when we are open to Him. He can write the most beautiful endings for even the most broken beginnings.

God,

thank You for healing parts of me that have been left depleted. You have renewed my spirit and given me a heart that overflows with rest and Your goodness. You have replenished my soul and filled me with Your power to withstand anything. May I always seek after You for my refuge and know I always have a safe place to come home to.

In Jesus's name, Amen.

REST

The Night Watch

In peace I will lie down and sleep,
for You alone, LORD, make me dwell in safety.
PSALM 4:8

She had learned a long time ago to leave her worries at the bedroom door at night. In fact, she had a tactic for visualizing doing just that. It was necessary. She was going to sleep, thank you very much. If God wanted her, He'd wake her up. Otherwise, though, the cares of today could be placed in their appropriate files and submitted for review by the Creator of the universe. The cares of tomorrow would be handed to her once she'd had her coffee. The night belonged to rest, restoration, and dreams.

How are you at letting things go each night? Are you a tosser and turner, a worrier? Or have you learned the art of good sleep? There are things that will help, like getting enough water, moving your body during the day, eating food that will strengthen you, and yes, thankfulness. Finding reasons to smile will also help. And at night, releasing anxious thoughts will help you drift into pleasant dreams. If you struggle with this, you might find it helpful to visualize letting go. As you picture each of the people or circumstances that has your thoughts, one by one you can imagine placing them into the hands of Jesus. He waits willingly, palms up, smiling. As you give each one over, you feel the weight of it leaving you and landing in His very capable grip. *Would You please work on this tonight and give me what I need of it tomorrow?* If one of those worries keeps coming back to you, keep returning it to Him. Eventually, your mind will be at peace. You can trust God while you sleep.

God,
in these quiet moments, I find myself full of gratitude knowing that my rest is found in You. You have helped me to trust in Your provision over my life and let go of the very things I have no control over. I pray that as I continue to be in Your presence, my heart is being renewed and refueled by Your strength.
In Jesus's name, Amen.

REST

May we spend
less time
on the image
we want to portray,
and more time
on the person
we actually are.

—HOSANNA WONG

PEACE

Peace That Prospers

"Peace I leave with you; My peace I give you. I do not give to you as the world gives. Do not let your hearts be troubled and do not be afraid."

JOHN 14:27

Nothing around her seemed peaceful. Anxious thoughts swirled, threatening to take her down. But one thing she had learned about Jesus is that His peace was not negotiable. It was always there for the taking, and all she had to do was agree to it. Not that receiving peace was always an instant calming force for her. She still wrestled with those thoughts and feelings. But somehow, knowing that the peace of heaven was with her made it so much easier to get through.

The Greek word *eiréné*, which we translate as "peace," is such a loaded concept. It can mean the absence of war. But it's the Greek equivalent of *shalom* in Hebrew, which has a lot more to do with richness, fulfillment, health, peace, and blessing. It's an all-encompassing word that implies spiritual abundance.

When Jesus said He was leaving peace with us, He didn't mean that war wouldn't happen. He meant that deep in our souls, where the eternal things live, there would be prosperity. Keeping that in mind helps when we go through hard times. We can always reach deep into the well of His love, knowing what really matters in the middle of it all. Things won't go perfectly, but we can have perfect peace. And our souls actually get stronger and more beautiful through the flames of trouble. When you find yourself in the fight, all you need to do to tap into His peace is to receive it. *Jesus, thank You for Your* eiréné, *peace.*

God,

thank You for always being there for me in the midst of every storm I've had to walk through. You have always shown up and reminded me that I'm never alone, even if I feel like I am. You continually provide me with Your comfort, shielding me with Your peace. May I be reminded of Your calming presence and allow that to quiet my heart.

In Jesus's name, Amen.

PEACE

When Peace Makes No Sense

Do not be anxious about anything, but in everything by prayer and supplication with thanksgiving let your requests be made known to God. And the peace of God, which surpasses all understanding, will guard your hearts and your minds in Christ Jesus.

PHILIPPIANS 4:6–7 ESV

There were times when she felt strong and courageous, but this was not that day. Right now she felt timid and small, unsure of how to move forward. Surely God had overestimated her abilities on this one. As soon as her thoughts began to spiral, she stopped herself. These weren't His thoughts in her mind; they were anxious ones. She began to pray, thanking Him for leading her here and for knowing how to get her through. She thanked Him for preparing her for just this moment. And with perhaps more boldness than she felt, she risked a step forward. And the peace came. And she knew it was going to work out great.

Have you ever had more peace about something than it made sense to have? Maybe you were considering a big move, a job change, or trying for another kid. So much emotion filled you that it was hard to know how to make a wise decision. Did you pray? And if so, did the decision come with that crazy-good peace? A sense of calm to your soul and a spark of hope that made you look forward to things you couldn't even imagine yet? Our faith strengthens in times just like these. We can't expect to grow if we aren't faced with obstacles to challenge us forward, with God beside us, supplying just enough grace to get us there. And when the miracle peace comes—a feeling that you have to experience to understand—we're never the same after that. Once we taste His goodness (Psalm 34:8), we can't untaste it. It makes the next risk, the next big decision, that much easier. The peace of Jesus changes us.

God,

in the midst of uncertainty, I know that I can rely on You. I know that no matter what, You are my anchor of peace. I pray that even in uncertainty, I will continue to have the courage to face whatever obstacle, knowing that with faith I am resilient.

In Jesus's name, Amen.

PEACE

What Fills Our Minds

You will keep in perfect peace
those whose minds are steadfast
because they trust in You.
ISAIAH 26:3

It took work on her part. She knew she had to fight against the fears and worries that clouded her thoughts. But sometimes it all just felt like more than she could do on her own. It helped to have a list of God's promises at the ready. She could turn to them in her Bible, write them on her mirror, and repeat them in her mind as often as needed—like a prescription for hope. She did her best to make her mind a resting place for His truth. And most of the time, it worked.

Our minds are more powerful than we think. What we put in them really matters. And just as importantly, the thoughts we entertain will make their home in our hearts if we let them. We have to be so careful. Lies can act like poison in the water, infecting everything else about us. For example, how do you talk to yourself when you look in the mirror? Are you kind or harsh? If you spoke to your kids or husband the way you talk to yourself, how would they feel? Do you make a conscious effort to think about things that are true, noble, right, and pure (Philippians 4:8) or do you succumb to slippery sarcasm or slander? Is it gratitude or gossip that fills you up? When you're intentional about keeping your mind steadfast and faithful, God can fill it with His peace and promises.

God,

may my thoughts be reflections of Your promises. In chaos, it's so easy to lose sight and start allowing anxious thoughts to cloud my mind, but You have given me peace that calms me. May I rest in knowing that You are in control. May I guard my thoughts and not allow the noise to distract me from trusting You.

In Jesus's name, Amen.

PEACE

Learning to Fall

May the God of hope fill you with all joy and peace as you trust in Him, so that you may overflow with hope by the power of the Holy Spirit.

ROMANS 15:13

She was learning to trust with abandon. Every time she was faced with uncertainty, she was practicing throwing herself into God's arms like a team-building trust fall activity. He caught her every time. Sometimes she missed in her aim and felt like she was free-falling for a bit in the wrong direction. But it never took Him long to rescue her, and they would set out together again.

When you finally get to the point of trusting God fully, life becomes so much more joyful. I'm not saying I'm there yet, but I'm learning. You've got to let your center of balance falter before He has a reason to catch you. And even though it can be scary, every time you make the effort to trust Him a little more, you'll find that He is faithful. It makes it all that much easier to trust Him the next time, with something just a little bigger or more important to you. There won't be a time in this life when you've ever arrived, having learned everything you can about God and how He operates. But you'll grow. You'll discover how much more fun it is when your hands are empty of the stiff controls and free to cup a flower so you can smell the sweet aromas along the path. Letting God lead has no downside. You'll only become wiser and more peaceful when you learn just how trustworthy He is.

God,
thank You for showing me that even in the midst of chaos, You are still God. When I'm impatient and try to force things, I'm reminded that You're an on-time God and my trust is lacking. May I give You control and stop trying to do everything on my own. I give my day over to You. I know that You will do what's best with what I leave in Your hands.
In Jesus's name, Amen.

PEACE

Unshakeable

Now may the Lord of peace Himself give you peace at all times and in every way. The Lord be with all of you.

II THESSALONIANS 3:16

She felt invincible. Not because she was a superhero or even supernaturally strong. It was because she knew where she stood. She watched people around her lose their balance and fall, turn to the ugly things that the world would offer. But her foundation was solid. The hand that reached out to hold her at all times belonged to the creator of the whole universe. And if she stumbled, He would steady her. Again and again. It wasn't easy, mind you. But He was steady and sure, so she could be too.

So many decisions face us each day. Especially in a season of big decisions, the opportunity to become confused or unsure seems so great. Do we choose according to our desires and ask God to bless us? Do we choose what we think will please Him? Do we wait to hear a very clear *yes* in one direction or the other? Or is it all of those options? Oh, boy! No wonder life feels so shaky sometimes. We don't need to fear, though. As children of God, we are headed toward a kingdom that can't be shaken (Hebrews 12:28). We might feel the heat, but we don't need to fear the fire because only the things that don't matter will burn away. We can go through life worshiping and thanking God, making the decision to glorify Him (I Corinthians 10:31), rejoicing and celebrating each day because He made it (Psalm 118:24), and knowing that our feet are set on solid ground when we trust in Him. With God, we aren't superheroes—but our Dad is.

God,
You are good all the time, even when my circumstances change. You provide and remain present even if I feel as though You're absent. What may feel like silence is a season when You have allowed me moments to be still and just listen. It's not always easy, but when trusting in Your timing leads me to growth, it creates a peace in me that becomes unshakeable.
In Jesus's name, Amen.

PEACE

Whom Do You Lean On?

Behold, God is my salvation;
I will trust, and will not be afraid;
for the Lord God is my strength and my song,
and He has become my salvation.
ISAIAH 12:2 NKJV

Sometimes the fear surprised her. When all was well, she had assumed she would walk bravely in the direction of her dreams. But when she was actually faced with certain obstacles, she was afraid. Where had that fear come from? She could do the work to find out, but what mattered most was that in this moment, she would turn to God in surrender. He would take her fears and calm her heart, reminding her that she wasn't alone in this. The fear wasn't fun, but it led her to Jesus. And for that she could be thankful.

Fear can be real. It can even be justified, because life can be scary! We know bad things happen, even when we put our whole trust in God and pray for protection. What we don't see are all the ways God is with us, protecting us, working out plans that will ultimately lead to beauty. It's not that fear is a sin, but holding on to it can be. So many times in the Bible we're told—even commanded—not to sin. Would God give us a command that we literally could not complete? More likely, He's so gracious that He promises to give us exactly what we need in the moment so that fear will flee and we can lean into His confidence. "Fear not, for I am with you," He says (Isaiah 41:10 NKJV). In what areas are you most likely to feel fear? How do you usually handle it? The next time you're fearful, be mindful about acknowledging it to God and asking Him to take it.

God,
I surrender my worries to You. Sometimes I don't understand what I have to go through, but I know for a fact You're protecting me. May I receive clarity and understanding when doubts try to cloud my mind, for Your timing is everything. I cling to that truth even in the midst of uncertainty. There's peace even if there's chaos all around me.
In Jesus's name, Amen.

PEACE

Facing the Sun

The Lord bless you and keep you;
the Lord make His face shine on you
and be gracious to you;
the Lord turn His face toward you
and give you peace.
NUMBERS 6:24–26

After a few dreary days, she smiled thankfully at the sun. She felt like a sunflower today. She lifted her face, eyes closed, toward the warmth of the light in the sky and thanked God for this feeling. If only she could stay here for another hour and bask in its healing rays. But she had things to do. So she asked God to stay with her and keep the warmth of His love on her all day long.

Something happens when the sun comes out, especially when you've been accustomed to cool or cloudy weather. Maybe it's why people flock to warmer climates in the winter: a bright and cloudless sky tends to calm us and invite us into a sense of rest. Could it be that the warm sun reminds our souls of the feeling we get when God's face shines on us? Moses knew it.

His face glowed after spending close time with God (Exodus 34:29). Knowing we have God's attention gives a sense of peace because we know how much He loves us and wants us to thrive. He offers to take our burdens at any time. Being with God means that someone else besides us—the busy, worn-out, weary, insecure women we can be—is truly in control and leading us well. That gives us room to let the tension leave our shoulders and our faces turn upward. When was the last time you sat in the warmth of the sun? Think of that the next time you see the sunshine outside and remember that the face of God is shining on you too.

God,

thank You for never giving up on me. You've carried me through some of the darkest seasons of my life. You have brought me so much joy when I felt hopeless, peace where there was distress. May You continue to protect me and my mind from drifting into places that are not covered by Your light.

In Jesus's name, Amen.

PEACE

The Guide Inside

But blessed is the one who trusts in the Lord, whose confidence is in Him.

JEREMIAH 17:7

She'd been through so much. It was a wonder that she was still standing, and with joy in her heart, no less. She didn't doubt for a second that it was due to God and His faithfulness through it all. She even knew that it was because of her willingness to cling to Him that she'd gotten this far. How in the world do people do it without Him? *she wondered. But deep down she knew that they didn't "do it" without Him. It was all or nothing, and she was willing to give Him her all.*

There was a time not too long ago when people on a road trip would need a paper map. Obviously it wasn't safe to read the map and drive, so either they had to memorize where to go, or they'd have to pull over when they weren't sure. They might also have a passenger who could navigate. But it was far different from how we do it today. Now we can type in the destination and a voice of our choosing points out the next directions. We listen and follow. In a way, using

GPS now is more like our journey with the Holy Spirit. Doing things on our own might be like glancing at a map and then trying to figure it out. Following His lead might be like listening for His voice, trusting His wisdom, and believing that a wonderful destination lies ahead. When hard things come, are you more likely to unplug the GPS and pull out the map so you can figure it out on your own? Or do you trust the Destination Maker? If you're holding on to something that you need to surrender today, let Him lead. Give Him a chance. He will not disappoint.

God,

thank You for helping me always navigate through life changes. There is not a doubt in my mind that You have carried me through some of the hardest challenges. You have guided me and allowed me to see the goodness of trusting in You. May I cling to this inner peace You have given me so I can fully walk in confidence and not in fear.

In Jesus's name, Amen.

PEACE

Trust His Process

They will have no fear of bad news;
their hearts are steadfast,
trusting in the Lord.
PSALM 112:7

It looked like a mess to her. She was watching the things she thought she could count on crumble into bits and disappear. Other things she didn't want were taking their place. And things she never dreamed of were starting to unfold. It was too soon to tell how it would all come together. But even though her world was in upheaval, she knew enough to hold on tight and pray. The peace would come where it should. The pieces would fall into place. And her God, once again, would surprise her with His brilliant ideas.

Have you ever been engaged and had it fall through? Have you lost an important friendship? Have you been pregnant . . . and then not? Have you seen your dreams drift away for reasons you didn't understand? The biggest wounds of life are horrible, and I'm truly sorry for whatever you lost in the process. At the same time, I know that the big losses hold a huge amount of potential for God to hand us a crown of beauty (Isaiah 61:3). I've been there. And while sometimes we can't bring ourselves to say that we would have it that way all over again, God gives us peace and even thankfulness for how we've grown through it all. It might take days, weeks, or years to see the fruit of terrible loss. But He promises to restore us (Deuteronomy 30:3; Joel 2:25). It's much less important to understand the whys than it is to keep our eyes on the Who. The Orchestrator of everything holds the answers, and He will not leave you in darkness.

God,
may I leave everything in Your hands, even the very things that I don't understand. Things may be falling out of place, but through You, everything is right how You want it. You know what I need, what I desire, every single detail. I trust You more than ever. May I stay close to You and let Your peace that surpasses all understanding keep my mind resting.
In Jesus's name, Amen.

PEACE

When Dreaming Feels Impossible

Jesus looked at them and said, "With man this is impossible, but with God all things are possible."
MATTHEW 19:26

She had a dream so big that she felt like it was impossible to even reach. She knew in her heart, God gave her this desire, this hunger, this passion, yet somehow it just felt like her dreams had been quieted to a whisper. She began to question whether her dreams were too big, whether she was even capable of continuing to dream.

There will be moments when you find yourself at the intersection of faith and doubt. Hopeful, yet somehow lacking in trust because defeat begins to creep in. You then start trying to force what God has not rushed, causing you frustration, and oftentimes confusion. It is so important to know the divine calling God has placed over your life. Every single dream God breathed will not be wasted. What He has planted in you will draw you closer to Him, develop your character, and glorify His name through each step you take down the path that He is lighting for you. You do not have to rush in to your calling. Listen to God's voice. Whatever season you are in, let Him guide you instead of letting your fears lead the way. Remember that God does not call the equipped; He equips the called. He just needs your yes.

God,
thank You for placing inside me dreams that have brought these desires that continue to stir in my heart. I know that lately my dreams have felt so impossible. I pray for a newness to awaken my desire to dream again. May my dreams be a testament of Your goodness. May this journey allow me to trust You even if I may not have the answers. I know that You turn the impossible to possible, and I'm believing You are the God of miracles.
In Jesus's name, Amen.

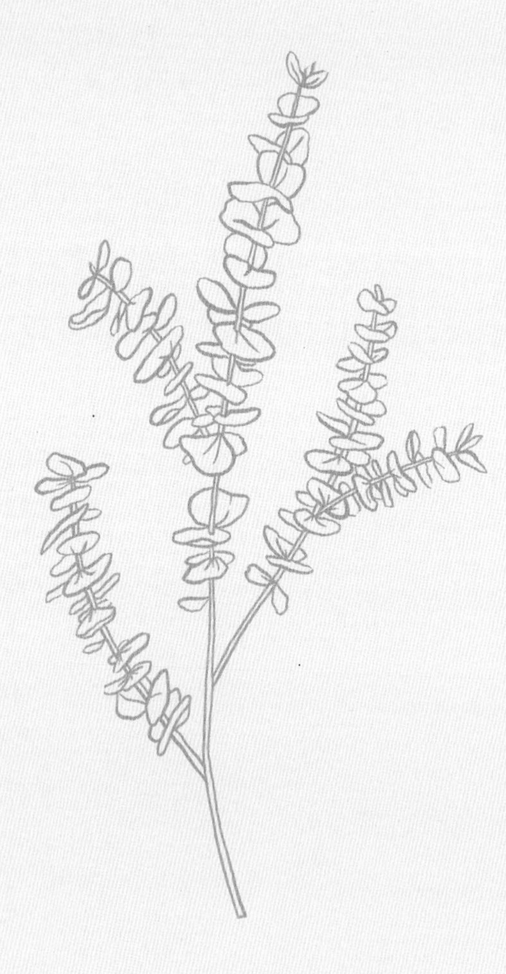

PEACE

Some people think
God does not like
to be troubled
with our constant
coming and asking.
The way to trouble God
is not to come at all.

—DWIGHT L. MOODY

TRUST

Faith Like Job

Trust in the Lord with all your heart
and lean not on your own understanding;
in all your ways submit to Him,
and He will make your paths straight.
PROVERBS 3:5–6

She had to fight for it sometimes, but she was determined to walk by faith. She wanted to trust God with everything in her. It had been a journey for sure. But He had shown Himself faithful again and again. The wonderful thing about trusting Him was that He would always lead her to exactly where she needed to be.

A lot of people can relate to Job during different seasons of their lives. Not that any of us has ever experienced the measure of loss that he did, from losing every one of his children to his entire income source and his health, while his friends accused him of displeasing God. But most of us have had a series of troubles that have seemed to build on each other. There comes a point where we think we won't be able to handle any more . . . and then the next trouble comes. The tension builds. The pain increases. We're faced with a crossroads moment when we'll either give up and try to fix things on our own or run hard toward Jesus. The only answer is His truth. Job gives such a good example of this. He may have wished he'd never been born, but he never turned away from God. In the end, he was rewarded for his trust that would not die. May we all do the same when we're faced with one trial after another.

God,
sometimes my heart feels overwhelmed with all the concerns that I have. But I know Your Word says not to lean on my own understanding, but in all my ways to acknowledge You and You shall direct my path. Today I'm asking that You direct each one of my footsteps and make me aware of Your presence. I trust that as You go before me, I can take delight in knowing that You will give me the desires of my heart.
In Jesus's name, Amen.

TRUST

Trusting in the Word

Trust in the Lord and do good;
dwell in the land and enjoy safe pasture.
Take delight in the Lord,
and He will give you the desires of your heart.
Commit your way to the Lord;
trust in Him and He will do this.

PSALM 37:3–5

God's way seemed best to her. Yes, distractions would get in the way sometimes. Her flesh would want things that God did not. But she still understood that following Him would lead to the greatest joy. So every day she opened the Word and got her words from His mouth. She hid it in her heart so that she would always be ready to defend what she knew to be true: that delighting in God was the best thing to do.

Something *happens* when you spend time in God's Word. You can read some Scripture and understand right away. But the more you dwell there, considering His truth and seeking His heart, you'll go deeper and deeper into who He is and who you are to Him. The written Word, *logos*, feeds your soul.

And His *rhema* word, spoken straight to you in the moment, encourages you right where you are. You can be reading something you've read a hundred times before, but on this particular day, it jumps off the page and hits you differently. It could be the sound of His voice for you, in this relevant moment, lifting you with wisdom and love. The only way to receive His voice like this is to be in the Word. Every day, feed yourself on the Word. Do you have a plan for this? Do you have a time of day or a reading schedule? When you put His Word first, you'll find that He is speaking way more often and more poignantly than you realize.

God,
help me to stand firm in all seasons in my life. May Your promises remind me that when I place my trust in You, I don't have to fear the outcome. I don't have to operate out of my own understanding. I know that You will make a way and be gracious as You work on my behalf.
In Jesus's name, Amen.

TRUST

Love That Can Be Trusted

But I have trusted in your steadfast love;
my heart shall rejoice in your salvation.
PSALM 13:5 ESV

She hadn't always known the kind of love that God could give. In fact, she had known the space where love was supposed to be and it was empty, and that had almost broken her. Or at times the love had come to her so darkened by sin and sorrow. But not with God—never with Him. His love was the purest and most faithful. He had found her, saved her, lifted her up, and shown her that love was worth fighting for. So she made it her goal to love like Jesus for the rest of her life.

On the days when the sin
and sorrow and brokenness of the world
seem to suffocate our souls . . .
In the times when we should feel
the most encouraged and cared for,
but only feel loss . . .
When the ones who love us
the most hurt us the most deeply . . .
there's God.

His love isn't bound by "supposed to" or "should." He doesn't count wrongs, keep track of offenses, or care if we're loving Him back. He loves. He *is* love. When you need a reminder or a fresh perspective, you can ask Him to show you. When your heart is overwhelmed, you can ask Him what His love looks like right now, in the moment. Then quietly wait, and He'll come with His arms open to show you. It might not change your circumstances. It might not even lessen the pain where others have let you down. But you'll be going through it with the Giver of all love, and that will soften the edges. God's love is indelible, and when you have it, it will mark you forever.

God,

I will wait patiently as I trust You. May You restore my spirit and mind as I am walking in this season. I pray that I can boldly walk in faith and not let fear keep me from seeking after the truth You have spoken over my life. I trust You and know that You will settle my spirit and show me exactly where I am supposed to be.

In Jesus's name, Amen.

TRUST

You Have a Place

Blessed is the man who trusts in the LORD, whose trust is the LORD.
JEREMIAH 17:7 NKJV

It wasn't in her nature to fight the crowd. She preferred to be accepted and approved. But there were times when her heart knew that the direction of her peers was not the direction God was asking her to go. And when she made that difficult choice, she could see the good and feel the blessing in following His will. She didn't always feel brave, but she was confident in God. And that made it all worthwhile.

It's strange how people can struggle so hard to be glad of their own paths, especially as they watch other people's lives from the outside. But just imagine what we could all accomplish if we accepted—fully *owned*—the identity we were born with. God has been training us for it from day one. Other stories are most appealing when we see the things we want for ourselves looking really good on someone else. A bigger bank account, for example. More (or fewer) children. Big-city life or small-town homesteading.

But you, friend, have a story written just for you, and no one else can play your role nearly as well as you can. In your hands, someone else's life would fit like a stretched-out sweater. It would look like *something*, but not a good thing. And your life in someone else's hands would fall flat. When you choose to accept the calling placed upon you, the world becomes a much, much better place.

God,
I admit sometimes it is really hard to let go and it can seem easier to figure out things on my own. I pray that no matter how I am feeling, or thinking, I can trust You with every decision I make. I don't want to stray away from Your will for my life. I ask that You order my steps and grant me the confidence to wholeheartedly trust in You with everything.
In Jesus's name, Amen.

TRUST

There's a Reason He Tells Us to Praise

When I am afraid, I put my trust in You.
In God, whose word I praise—
in God I trust and am not afraid.
What can mere mortals do to me?
PSALM 56:3–4

You know what she had learned? That praising first was one of the best ways to strengthen her spirit. Thanking God before seeing the outcome so often put courage and hope in the place of fear and worry. Gratitude was the key to the gates of His presence. Praise swung the door wide open into His love. With that kind of head start, she figured she would never fail again.

One of the most natural feelings in the world is to turn inward when we're unsure. We search our own list of capabilities to see how we're going to get through this. We check our own emotions, most of the time just finding ourselves more confused and off-balance. But that's not what God calls us to do.

Someone once said that introspection is dangerous without the Holy Spirit, because our assessment is so off base most of the time. But the Holy Spirit speaks truth. Not only that, but He also tends to provide exactly what we need at the exact time we need it. When you're faced with something new and potentially impossible, think back on times when you were struggling and got through. What helped you make it? Yourself? Your hustle? Or something besides you that orchestrated the whole deal? Chances are, you'll find something to praise Him for and trust Him for in the future.

God,
thank You for being a Father who cares for my every need. When I feel like I am lacking and don't have enough, You constantly remind me that I am taken care of. In moments when I am afraid and don't know the outcome, I can look back on all the times You have shown up and carried me through every situation. You are a God of faith in whom I can fully put my trust.
In Jesus's name, Amen.

TRUST

What We Haven't Seen

Surely God is my salvation;
I will trust and not be afraid.
The LORD, the LORD Himself,
is my strength and my defense;
He has become my salvation.
ISAIAH 12:2

This wasn't suffering, she knew. In all, she had a pretty amazing life. But why were her emotions all over the place? Why did she feel so unsteady on her feet and unsure in her heart? She wanted to cower and back away. Instead, she paused. Took a breath. And decided that this would be a chance she would take to tell God how much she trusted Him. Then she would wait in His reassurance and believe He would show her the way.

Do you ever take time to think about all of the ways and times that God has probably come to your aid? Are there accidents that didn't happen, relationships that didn't fail, hopes that weren't dashed, rewards that came, or gifts that overwhelmed you? It's so hard to put ourselves in that perspective because, well, we don't know what we don't know. We can only read about God's defense of us and advocacy for us in the Word and observe what we see in the world or in our own lives. But what if God suddenly pulled back the curtain into the things we don't see, allowing us to look back on our lives from behind the scenes? We would be shocked. Stunned. His loving care would tumble down through our memories and seasons. We would never doubt His care for us again. So, why doesn't He do just that? Maybe because He wants us to focus on the here and now. Maybe He's been clearing away distractions—good and bad—so that we could live life with our eyes on the things that would best help us see Jesus in the middle of it all.

God,

thank You for being my Rock and my solid Foundation. You have been my strength in moments when I felt like I couldn't make it. You have held me up and covered me with Your protection, and for that, I will continue to trust You and not be afraid. I know that I am safe in Your arms, safe in Your presence.

In Jesus's name, Amen.

TRUST

Wisdom That's Worth It

I will say of the Lord,
"He is my refuge and my fortress,
my God, in whom I trust."
PSALM 91:2

Sometimes she needed to be saved from herself. Not because she meant harm. But because even in her best attempts, she was prone to self-sabotage and silly choices. She was like a deer stuck in a fence that, when it was freed, turned around to flee and tangled itself right back up in that fence again. No thinking involved, just actions. It rarely went well. Thankfully, her God was so patient and persistent. She would get there, she knew. One day at a time in His arms.

Wisdom is a gift from God. He even says that if we ask for it, He will give it (James 1:5). Wisdom is His way of maturing us through experience. Of course, to gain wisdom, we have to walk through some things that give us experience, and that can be very uncomfortable. We have to learn what it feels like to lose, to hurt, to fail. We have to know the difference between ending up on top or flat on our faces. Fortunately He is a gentle Teacher. He has pep talks and promises for us along the way. Even in the inevitable, He stays close and offers the wisdom that will guide us better next time and give us a way to comfort those who are experiencing similar things (II Corinthians 1:4). We could avoid some of the things we go through with Him if we wanted to stay ignorant, but that wouldn't be living to the fullest with Christ. His way is rarely easy. But learning to lean on God instead of our own understanding will lead to wisdom that's worth it.

God,

I trust in You with all my heart. May I not lean on my own understanding but look to You for wisdom and strength. In all my ways, may I acknowledge You and honor You with my life. I pray as I continue to walk by faith and obedience, You will guide my every step and lead me on a path of righteousness.

In Jesus's name, Amen.

TRUST

Whom Shall I Fear?

Fear of man will prove to be a snare,
but whoever trusts in the LORD is kept safe.
PROVERBS 29:25

She had gotten more courageous over time. It was never fun or easy to have hard conversations, or even make choices of aesthetics or life decisions that didn't line up with what her friends or family thought. Yet here she was, more sure of herself and of God. She hadn't imagined that one benefit of following Jesus would be finding herself in the process.

We've all had that feeling before a big moment. Maybe that moment was your role in the church play, a speech in debate class, or confronting a friend who was sinning. Maybe you bought a new couch and wondered what your mom would think of it. Whatever your moments have been, they've come at you with stomach butterflies and the invitation to be afraid of what others would think. You might have been tempted to modify your opinion or your presentation because it would have seemed less controversial, felt less vulnerable. But did you stay the course? Did you follow through? If you caved, even a little, did you regret it, or were you glad? The fear of man is real, and it affects us all. We might need to experience letting it win once in a while to remind us that it doesn't feel great. On the other hand, we really need to experience trusting God in the big moments so we can feel the true peace of partnering with Him in hard things. The next time you face a butterfly-inducing challenge, go straight to Him with your requests. You might just receive more than you ever expected.

God,
it is written that those who seek the Lord lack no good thing. I pray that as I continue to pursue You and keep my focus on You alone, I find contentment in knowing I don't lack anything. You have provided everything I've ever needed. You are faithful, and I can't thank You enough. May I keep my eyes fixed on You and trust that I am kept safe in You.
In Jesus's name, Amen.

TRUST

Where Humans Fail

It is better to take refuge in the Lord than to trust in humans.

PSALM 118:8

This was a familiar fear. Her hand reached up to clutch her chest. It was an instinctive move, and she laughed to herself as she remembered that she'd gone through it a thousand times and survived. What can man do to me? *she thought, as she stepped forward. She knew that whatever plan God had would not fail. And no matter the outcome, she'd rather be known as someone who trusted Him radically than someone who didn't act because she was afraid of failure. Her smile this time was genuine.*

I hope you grew up in a home that knew the love of God. I hope you thrived there. I hope your parents—both of them—nurtured you well and met all of your needs. I hope you learned about Jesus best through them. But if not, you are in good company. The shortcomings of the ones who raised us are expected and completely normal. Sometimes that is tragic. Sometimes it is simply frustrating. But we know one thing, and that's that God will take your ashes and turn them into something truly beautiful (Isaiah 61:3). Where God is perfect in every way, man is a mess of misguided intentions. He accounted for that. Even as you wrestle to understand the good of the pain you've known, He knows that you are learning to hide yourself in His love. Where those who should have nurtured you missed the mark, He is turning your gaze toward the shadow of His wings (Ruth 2:12). Humans will fail, but God will heal.

God,
as I navigate through today, I am praying for Your protection. May You continue to guard my mind and spirit as I trust in You. There are times when it feels impossible to release control, but I know that if I take refuge in You, You will take care of everything. I don't have to let worry and stress control me. I can rest and be assured that what You are doing in my life is purposeful.
In Jesus's name, Amen.

TRUST

What the World Won't Do

The Lord is good, a refuge in times of trouble. He cares for those who trust in Him.

NAHUM 1:7

The way she saw it, there were two choices, and only one of them was valid. The first choice would be to strike out on her own, with common sense, using the advice of culture and people and social media and podcasts to guide her way. Eventually, she would burn herself out and beat herself down, or be beaten down, by a world that didn't really care about her at all. No, the other option was what she would choose. She would carefully submit herself and her plans to God. He might lead her differently than she wanted and give her situations she didn't expect—but He would care for her infinitely. And that made it all worthwhile.

What do we all long for, anyway? To be loved. We want to feel the heartfelt care of someone who longs to know us and be near us. We were wired that way by the One who created our lives and bodies for that very purpose. He gives us people—spouses, parents, friends, children—who can reflect His heart for us in these ways. But in the end, they all miss something about our needs, and that is on purpose too. No human is meant to fill your void for love. They'll help. They might be specialized. But only God can go to the deep places and know the deepest longings of your soul. The more you lay down your desire for people to be everything for you, the more you'll experience His desire to care for you down to the tiniest detail. Give Him a chance, and you will thrive.

God,

strengthen me as I trust in You. Even in moments that don't make sense and are hard for me to understand, I pray that I can fully hand my concerns to You. May I be reminded that You are good and everything good comes from You. I won't allow fear to tear me away from what You have ahead for me.

In Jesus's name, Amen.

TRUST

I will not exalt myself
with anxiety.
I will humble myself
in peace and joy
as I trust this
precious and great
promise of God—
He cares for me.

—JOHN PIPER

PRAYER

The God for All Seasons

But as for me, it is good to be near God.
I have made the Sovereign Lord my refuge;
I will tell of all Your deeds.
PSALM 73:28

She always felt her strongest after prayer. She could sit in the car, in a classroom, or on a park bench; she could pray while jogging or grocery shopping; she did not need a pew or holy music (although she prayed with those things too). Prayer was a form of breathing with her, and every breath brought her life.

You can try to do life without God. You can work hard, try to achieve, buy nice things, and even give your time and money away on occasion. But if you don't have Him to fall back on, you'll eventually burn out with nothing that matters to show for it. Life isn't meant to be done alone. Friends, circumstances, and even family members might come and go, but God is forever and always. He's a Companion in lonely times and a Counselor in confusing times. He leads you through decisions and cheers you on when things are going great. He'll even hold you close when you're hurting. Making God your refuge means knowing that He's a safe place to be, at all times. There will never be a time when you can't count on that and look to Him for answers. If God is your refuge, you'll be okay. Take a minute to talk with Him right now. What weighs you down? What lifts you up? What's on your mind? It all matters to Him, and He loves working through life with you.

God,
thank You for life. I thank You that I can cast all my cares on You because You care. You know everything that is in my heart before I even think of it. I ask that You would help me align my life with Your will. I don't want to operate without communicating with You first. May You continue to mold and shape me into who You have called me to be.
In Jesus's name, Amen.

PRAYER

Making the First Move

"You will seek Me and find Me when you seek Me with all your heart."
JEREMIAH 29:13

In the heat of the moment, sometimes she forgot the order of things. Like the fact that God promised to draw near to her when she first drew near to Him (James 4:8). Or that she would find Him if only she would start seeking. As soon as she remembered, she would look for Him in whatever situation she found herself. And instantly, God would feel closer.

At times when our hearts are busy processing the things going on around us, God isn't always at the top of our mind. He is a gentleman, waiting until we're ready to give Him attention before He jumps in. Of course, this isn't always the case. He is a rescuer. When we need saving, He will be there. At times He comes without our asking. But when we find ourselves aching for His comfort, presence, or peace—when wisdom seems elusive—God is just a prayer away. It takes focus. It takes faith. It takes a mindful pause in the middle of the fray to settle our hearts, turn in

His direction, and intentionally invite Him into our circumstances. Are you accidentally leaving God out of something today? Would you benefit from having Him closer and more involved? Have you drawn near to Him through the Word and prayer, and have you been seeking Him in the matter? If not, take some time today. Determine what your heart needs from Him, and just ask. Look for promises in Scripture and make room for Him to speak. You won't regret it.

God,
soften my heart and mind to hear and sense Your Spirit. Prayer is a gift that I often take for granted. I ask that You forgive me for that and shape my mind to be in constant communication with You. I want to learn more about You. I want to go deeper with You. Teach me how to draw near and stay connected to You.
In Jesus's name, Amen.

PRAYER

When All Else Has Failed

The Lord is near to all who call on Him, to all who call on Him in truth.

PSALM 145:18

Oh, she ached. Trying to keep it all together had just about torn her apart. For all the effort she had put into creating her own narrative, it seemed to be unravelling at the seams. It took her a while. But she finally figured out that it was her own unwillingness to be honest with herself and with God that was keeping her in peril. So she told God everything. She gave Him her vulnerability. And in turn, He gave her grace and mercy. And it all turned out okay.

Ask yourself some questions, friend: What are you trying to hide? What are you trying to prove? What image are you trying to maintain, even though it wears you thin and keeps you from being completely truthful with yourself or others? And . . . is it all worth it? Have you tried being honest with God? Have you tried giving Him every single ounce of your failed efforts, tears, transparency, confusion, and brokenheartedness? He can take it all, and in fact,

He wants to. He watches you swimming upstream, trying to make things happen. But you are not a salmon. You're meant to swim in His living waters, letting the Holy Spirit guide your efforts in a way that will create an amazing Kingdom impact and actually restore your energy and hope. Being still is definitely an endangered art, but please try it today: Sit down somewhere quiet, close your eyes, and open your heart to God. Confess every effort you've been making that has worn you weary. You will grow stronger. You'll make way for the peace that passes understanding (Philippians 4:7), and a wonderful side effect is that you and God will grow closer than ever.

God,
prayer is evidence that You hear the cries of Your people. Thank You for listening to me and always working on my behalf. As I focus on building our relationship, please strengthen my prayer life and sensitivity to the Holy Spirit. I want to operate out of hearing from You and drowning out the noise of others.
In Jesus's name, Amen.

PRAYER

When the Fog Clears

Therefore confess your sins to each other and pray for each other so that you may be healed. The prayer of a righteous person is powerful and effective.

JAMES 5:16

Timidly she stepped toward the prayer team at church. It wasn't like her to tell others what was going on. But she confessed how she'd stumbled, and they prayed. They embraced her with love. The embarrassment she was feeling was only temporary, she reminded herself, and not an indication of how God was feeling about things. In fact, she knew He was pleased with her. She could feel His smile. And as she went to sit back down, she felt lighter. Okay, God, *she said.* Time to move forward.

The devil is a wily creature. He celebrates when shame and embarrassment rule our decisions. It's how he wins battles: Not because he's stronger, smarter, or more well-equipped. He wins when we allow feelings and attitudes to affect our willingness to fight. We're never doing battle against real people, but with the devil's desire to destroy us from the inside out (Ephesians 6:12). Shame can't hurt us any more than fog can. But fog can dim our vision so that we can't see potential dangers, and shame can cloud our understanding of who we are in Christ and what weapons of worship we have at our fingertips. I think that's partly why God wants us to confess our sins to one another. When we do not bring to light whatever wants to hide in the fog of shame, we won't act as boldly or confidently for Jesus. Shame cripples us, where forgiveness and truth strengthen us beyond words. Sometimes it takes another believer to come alongside us and pray when we're weak. And that can be a beautiful thing, working together with another warrior. Don't be ashamed, friend. Fight for grace and truth.

God,
prayer is a powerful weapon that You have gifted me with, and I am forever grateful. Even when I sometimes don't know where to start with prayer, Your Word says the Holy Spirit intercedes on my behalf. As I stay connected to You, I pray the Holy Spirit continues to live in me.
In Jesus's name, Amen.

PRAYER

Loyal Love

He fulfills the desires of those who fear Him; He hears their cry and saves them.

PSALM 145:19

This wasn't your ordinary friendship. It was the kind of relationship that was one hundred percent reliable, always available, and completely fulfilling in every way. She knew that a husband, a sibling, a parent, or another friend would never be all that this friendship was—and none of them were meant to be. With Jesus, she was totally protected and utterly loved.

We spend our whole lives longing for loyalty. We expect it of our spouse. We need it from our parents. We rejoice when we find it in our friends. But through all of that, we have a Friend who sticks closer than a brother (Proverbs 18:24), but for some reason, we tend to take Him for granted. Have you ever had a season of running away? It might have been before or after you became a Christian, but at that time you knew you were searching for something that didn't seem to be present. Whatever you ran to, it did not pan out. In fact, it was painful. But when you finally got to the end of your rope and looked up—didn't you find a face filled with the most amazing love looking down at you? Wasn't He holding His hand out to you, like He did for Peter, who was splashing around after he tried walking on water? Didn't you reach up and grasp that warm, big hand with relief? Didn't you spend time healing in His arms? God has never given up on you, and He never will. He's there forever, no matter what. He's the Friend you've always wanted.

God,
thank You for always having ears to hear my cries and communicate with me through prayer. Thank You for always listening to me even when I feel like I don't have much to say. You have always taken the time to make known that You see and hear me. And for all the times I've drifted from You, You have always welcomed me back with open arms. I pray that my eyes and ears will be open just like Yours so I can receive what You have for me.
In Jesus's name, Amen.

PRAYER

A Heart Prepared for Goodness

Search me, God, and know my heart;
test me and know my anxious thoughts.
See if there is any offensive way in me,
and lead me in the way everlasting.
PSALM 139:23–24

She'd seen enough in life to know what she wanted, and what she wanted was all the goodness of God. Sometimes it hurt to give Him the distractions and entertainments that filled the hole in her heart for a while. In fact, she was still struggling to release her grip on a couple of those. But she'd found that He was faithful to love her through those times, gently working out her kinks and transforming her more and more into something beautiful.

Once you've tasted the goodness of God, you can't ever forget it. It's the meal you want to go back for again and again, reliving the feeling of it on your tongue and telling anyone who will listen about what you had. Hopefully it's a meal we taste over and over again in our lives with Jesus. The goodness of God is readily available. It comes through every path of life. It comes through sorrow and trouble, through generous love and kindness, forgiveness, illness, loss, and grief. His goodness is everywhere because He is good. Usually, it's only our own attitude or thought pattern that keeps us from experiencing it. Those of us who have tasted it know well enough that it's worth letting Him search our hearts and reveal the areas of hardness that need softening—because only a soft, pliable heart can receive God fully. Only after we let the Holy Spirit work out our stubborn spots can we see all of His goodness. When you open your heart to Him in prayer today, don't be afraid to let Him in all the way. It'll be so good.

God,

deepen my desire to draw closer to You. May my heart be open to being in complete communion with You. When I am in Your presence, there I receive joy and peace. I pray for the eagerness to sit in Your presence and learn from You. Even in life's busyness, I can be still and hear from You. May You be a priority, not my last resort.

In Jesus's name, Amen.

PRAYER

Making Room

"Then you will call on Me and come and pray to Me, and I will listen to you."
JEREMIAH 29:12

It had been a long time in coming. The season of life had pulled her into its depths. She'd been almost lost in the mess. Her prayers had been brief—breaths, really—released between the heaves of hard work and emotion. But now, she could feel her spirit slowing. She was tired. It didn't matter if things weren't completely settled, and in fact, she was pretty sure she needed God even more now to help resolve it all. It was time to turn to Him with her whole heart.

Isn't it so strange how when life seems to be going well, we turn less to God? Praise and thanks don't roll as easily off the tongue as our cries and pleas do. But there's never a moment when God isn't waiting. He's on the hilltop just as fully as He's in the valley. He rejoices with us and mourns with us, always full of love. He isn't the one who creates distance. Sometimes He's quieter, but always with good reason. He's never far. You and I have to do our work too. We have to be intentional about loving God well in order to enjoy

Him fully. Life in Jesus requires effort just like the other things we apply ourselves to in daily life. We have to live in the aim of His love. We have to walk by faith. We have to pray, be careful what we watch or whom we listen to, and make Him our top priority. When we do we're paving a path for our prayers to reach His ears and for His answers to touch our hearts. In all seasons, God is with us.

God,

set a fire within my heart to stay connected to You through prayer. Forgive me for the days when I have disconnected myself due to busyness rather than seeking You first above all else. I pray that as I continue to deepen my faith and our relationship, You will continue to show me fresh, new ways to worship You, fresh, new ways I can learn more about You. May this season be a season of going deeper.

In Jesus's name, Amen.

PRAYER

Hydration

As the deer pants for streams of water,
so my soul pants for You, my God.
My soul thirsts for God, for the living God.
When can I go and meet with God?

PSALM 42:1–2

It was a nagging, dull ache in her—a longing sort of like hunger, but in a way she couldn't quite figure out. She just felt restless. It had been coming on for several days now. When she realized what she'd been missing, she almost laughed to herself. Her phone had been a constant companion lately, edging out the time she was accustomed to spending in prayer with God. Her Bible sat on her nightstand unopened. She was hungry, *in a way—she was hungry to be with God.*

We've all been thirsty. Sometimes it comes gradually, like after spending a morning outside. Sometimes it hits fast, like during intense exercise. They say that once we feel the sensation of thirst, we've waited too long. Instead we're supposed to be hydrating ourselves regularly, getting enough water and eating enough healthy foods with water content, so that we never actually feel thirsty. How is your hydration? More importantly, how is your spiritual hydration—quenched only through the living water of God (John 4:14; 7:38)? As believers, we never have to feel soul-thirsty. But sometimes we drop the ball, so to speak. We let our prayer lives lapse and our time in the Word become an unchecked box on our task lists. There comes a point for believers where we figure out what that depressed, downtrodden desperation is. It's simply our thirst for Him.

God,
when I feel disconnected, may I draw near to You. Prayer is what keeps me going, and sometimes when I start to drift, I find myself longing to seek after You. May my heart always have a posture of worship and gratitude. Prayer is a gift, and I don't want to take for granted the time and intimacy that I get to have with You. I pray that as I continue to seek after You, my heart's desires begin to match Yours. I want to stay connected to You in everything I do.
In Jesus's name, Amen.

PRAYER

What Keeps Us Close

Devote yourselves to prayer,
being watchful and thankful.
COLOSSIANS 4:2

Prayer was her lifeline. She came back to it again and again. Sometimes it was a dedicated time on her knees, in her closet. Other times it was a quick breath in an urgent situation. Most often, though, prayer was an open connection between God and her. He was near to her like any other person. She might forget He was present sometimes, but she would always come back to that mental place where God was her constant companion. It felt so nice.

In Colossians 4:2, the Greek word for "devote" is *proskartereo*. One way to define this word is *to adhere closely to a person*. Isn't that interesting? The Scripture is talking about a thing, prayer. But the word can mean a Person, God. Maybe the two are more related than we realize. I think of a three-legged race, where two people are tied together from the hip down and they have to run in step and side by side. When you're talking about two people, nothing can be closer than adherence. No air between them. No space for separation; glued together. Prayer might be considered the glue that keeps us adhered to God. Where He goes, we go. What He says, we hear. And of course, what we say, He hears. Matthew 11:30 says that we can yoke up with Jesus and let Him lead, and that's the perfect picture for what prayer does when we make it our lifestyle with Him. How are you at praying? Is it an every moment thing? An everyday thing? Or only at church on Sundays? Prayer is an important way we stay devoted to God.

God,

thank You for always being so consistent, even when I haven't always been. Life sometimes has distracted me from my priority of being in constant communion with You. May I learn to have the discipline to make my prayer life sacred and consistent, and not allow the distractions around me to keep me from having a healthy relationship with You. May I always find my way back to You.

In Jesus's name, Amen.

PRAYER

The Sacred Space

Seek the Lord while He may be found; call on Him while He is near.

ISAIAH 55:6

She constantly had to evaluate the center of her affections. It was fun, yes, to have delights and joys in life. Pumpkin spice lattes and a really good television series had their place, for sure! But were they her everything? Sometimes she felt something slipping into that sacred space in her heart. When she did, she tried her best to shift her focus away from what was meant as a decoration of life and back toward the biggest purpose, which was loving Jesus.

Affection is a powerful word. It implies not just attention and care, but an emotional attachment and a level of vulnerable truth that only few people or things can have in a person's life. There's a lot that we can care about or for, but not much that can have a very special place in our hearts. Affection has a playfulness, a delight to it. And God wants to be at the heart of your affection, just as you are a part of His. A relationship with God is sacred space. It's as holy as taking off your shoes to show Him honor and as tender as giving Him your most heartbroken tears. Where are your affections today? Is there anything vying for that sacred space belonging to God? If so, you can show Him, and the two of you can work through it together. If your affection is wholly on God today, relish it. He is so beautiful to gaze upon.

God,

forgive me for the times when I have neglected spending time with You. I know these moments spent with You are sacred, yet somehow I allow my own agenda to keep me from drawing near. May my desire for intimacy with You outweigh my desire to mark things off my to-do list. You are what I long for, what my heart desires. May I align my heart with Yours and allow You to guide me.

In Jesus's name, Amen.

PRAYER

I would rather repeat
my prayer to God
a thousand times
than let the devil
enjoy my silence.

—ANONYMOUS

SOLITUDE

When the World Is Loud

"Be still, and know that I am God;
I will be exalted among the nations,
I will be exalted in the earth."
PSALM 46:10

It always surprised her, after she had done it, that it hadn't occurred to her sooner. Slowing down. Being still. Remembering—intentionally recalling—the goodness of God in her life. Just a simple breath in, a sigh, a few moments of considering God, and she was restored. It always gave her the perspective she needed, which was that she herself was not *God. She was His child, beloved, named, seen, and known.*

How can you know what God is saying unless you make room for His voice? Sometimes we pray as though we're in the food court in the mall at Christmastime, straining to hear the people we're sitting at the table with while all the noise of the world happens around us. Sometimes we ask God a question while running at full speed, not sticking around long enough to hear if there's an answer. Sometimes our own unbelief or sin stands in the way of what He would say. But how can we expect to hear Him while we're intentionally holding Him at arm's length, protecting ourselves or our own shortcomings because we're too stubborn or scared to surrender? God isn't stingy with His love, not at all. But He's also not going to compromise and allow us to give Him less than our whole selves. He knows what we need most, and that's to sit at His feet like Mary Magdalene, opening ourselves to His instruction and care. To mindfully come to Him openhanded, allowing the less-important things to slip through our fingers while He pours in grace, forgiveness, wisdom, and peace. Come to God, and He will come near to you.

God,

in the solitude I find with You, draw me into deeper intimacy. Remove the veils that separate us and let our connection be profound. As I share my heart with You, may I also listen attentively to Your whispers of love. In this sacred solitude, may the exchange of our spirits be a dance of profound closeness, shaping me more into Your likeness.

In Jesus's name, Amen.

SOLITUDE

Staying Connected

Very early in the morning,
while it was still dark,
Jesus got up, left the house
and went off to a solitary place,
where He prayed.

MARK 1:35

She had to fight pretty hard against her flesh, which wanted sleep or entertainment or other distractions. Against the demands of her schedule, which often yelled at her that there simply wasn't time. Against the allure of more immediate payoffs. Still, she knew that consistent time alone with God would feed her soul and strengthen her spirit like nothing else. Every day, wherever she could, she gave Him space. And she never, ever regretted it.

Scripture gives us several examples of times when Jesus went off to be alone with His Father. And whatever you've heard about having a nicely packaged little devotional time each morning, devoting your night to prayer, or anything else, you can let those ideas stop guilt-tripping you. Jesus was not consistent with the time of day, nor does the Bible say a thing about Him going to the local bookstore and picking up a devotional on the book of Isaiah. In Matthew 14:23, Jesus went up on a mountain in the afternoon and stayed there until evening. In Mark 6, He fed the crowd with loaves and fishes, said goodbye to His disciples, then went off to pray. Mark 1:35 says that He got up while it was still dark and went off to pray alone. Even when His schedule wanted Him elsewhere, Jesus made time and space for what mattered most. His constant connection allowed Him to know what the Father was doing and how Jesus could partner with Him. That's what He wants from us too. When we stay connected, we have a sense of His heart. Abiding in the vine makes us our very best selves.

God,

thank You for being a safe place I can go and just breathe. You don't ask anything of me; You just let me rest in Your presence. You give my spirit the ability to let go as You renew and restore. May I always know I can find refuge in the secret place spent with You. I pray that I stay close to You as You strengthen me.

In Jesus's name, Amen.

SOLITUDE

In All Times and Places

After He had dismissed them,
He went up on a mountainside by Himself to pray.
Later that night, He was there alone.
MATTHEW 14:23

She was thankful for the things that brought her to her knees. Things that she would never wish on anyone and never ask to have happen, because they reminded her to turn to the One with all the answers. Sometimes it took those earthshaking circumstances to bring her low before God. And she never wanted to forget that He would be there, no matter what, as long as she needed Him.

When all is well and we feel like we're thriving, it's easy to live like we're soaring, feeling the wind in our hair and the sun on our face, thinking that on some level we've made it happen for ourselves. And absolutely, hard work is one thing we're called to do. But what happens when we put in the work and end up in the valley? Or we find ourselves in a situation that we simply cannot get out of ourselves? Has God changed somehow? Does He love us when we're living large and despise us when we're feeling small and alone? No, my friend. God doesn't change (James 1:17). He lifts our wings when we're soaring and lightens the load when we're sinking. Our efforts make a difference, but they aren't what bring us favor. Cultivating a relationship with God will help us to understand our place with Him, where circumstances are so much less important than our heart position. Hopefully we'll thank Him in all circumstances (I Thessalonians 5:16–18) and recognize that sometimes the low, dark places are a gift to remind us that we need Him in all times and all places.

God,

sometimes it can feel like the world is caving in on me. Darkness wants to overcrowd my space. May I be reminded of Your Word in Psalm 27:1, that You are "my light and my salvation—whom shall I fear?" When darkness wants to isolate me, I know Your light shines and overpowers it. I know that I am never alone because You are there holding my hand, comforting me. May I always be reminded of Your love for me.

In Jesus's name, Amen.

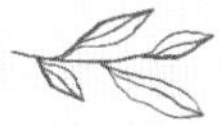

SOLITUDE

Alone and Content

But Jesus often withdrew to lonely places and prayed.

LUKE 5:16

Loneliness, she'd come to realize, had little to do with being around other people. She could be in a room full of friends and feel lonely. And she could be alone all day and feel more connected than ever. So, what was the variable? For her it was Jesus. The more sure she was of her identity in Christ, the more content she was to be who she was, where she was, whomever she was with.

Have you ever been lonely in a crowded room? Or at a family gathering? If you know loneliness, it's probably based on your desire to be seen and known in a personal way. It's not wrong to have those desires, because it's the way God made each of us—to be cared about and connected to those we care about. Loneliness is distinctly different from being alone. Being alone is also something we're made for. Time with God alone is sacred time, when He gets us all to ourselves and reveals Himself to us in really personal ways. We all have unique makeups. How He relates to you is going to be different from how He relates to me. It's in the sacred solitude that we build trust in Him and experience His singular pleasure toward us. And in the solitude, we learn to communicate honestly and effectively with Him. What about you? Do you confuse being alone with loneliness? Aloneness is a gift, and loneliness is something you can give to Him in your solitude. He'll do something beautiful with both.

God,
it is in Your goodness that I find myself resting in Your presence. You have shown Your faithfulness countless times. May I continue to trust You and not my own thoughts. May my mindset change to reflect more of You and less of me, as I walk in the Spirit and not in my flesh. I pray that as I remain close to You, I will continue to pray fervently.
In Jesus's name, Amen.

SOLITUDE

Creation Speaks of God

Truly my soul finds rest in God;
my salvation comes from Him.
Truly He is my rock and my salvation;
He is my fortress, I will never be shaken.
PSALM 62:1–2

She started making a point to spend time outside all year round. In the summer, she soaked up the sun, enjoying the fullness of the flowers and trees and the coolness of water. In autumn, she marveled at the changing leaves as they crunched underfoot. In winter, she donned fuzzy boots and happily endured the crisp air on her cheeks. In spring, she thanked God for blossoms and bright hope.

David was a shepherd long before he was a king. Shepherding, in David's time, was not a group activity. He would spend better parts of the year in solitude outdoors, enduring the weather and watchfully protecting his father's flock. So, what did he do while the sheep grazed or slept? David did a lot of writing. He wrote what he observed. He spoke of the glittering stars, the roaring waters, and the towering stone formation around him. And in the midst of creation, David confidently wrote of God's greatness. Much of the imagery he used to describe God had to do with the wonders of nature around him because that's what he knew best. He had the Torah, and he had the world around him, and with those things David was sure of whom he followed, even as his sheep followed him. What do you use to know God? Do you read the Word, spend time in nature, and surround yourselves with others who are seeking Him? If you do, you're setting yourself up to sing His praises in the most meaningful ways.

God,
thank You for being my shelter, my safe place. You have always been there for me even when I've drifted from You. You reassure me to find rest in You alone. May my hope come from You, as You lead me through whatever I am facing. I want to listen to Your voice as it's calling out for me. May I cling to this truth of You being both my rock and my salvation.
In Jesus's name, Amen.

SOLITUDE

He Is God

The Lord is in his holy temple;
let all the earth be silent before Him.
HABAKKUK 2:20

Looking back, she could trace the hand of God on her life. His mark was unmistakable. Even before she confessed her love for Him, He was lovingly present around her. Even in the hard things. Even in her pain. In her joy and celebration, connectedness or confusion, God was the Conductor of an intricate orchestra of which she was a small but essential part. Looking back reminded her of His bigness, and it made her excited to see where He was going to take her next.

He is the God who sits in heaven on a radiant throne. He is the One with angels surrounding Him, worshiping constantly and eternally in His presence. He is the One whose fingertips hold the threads to a trillion stars. He tips the earth this way and that, sloshing the sea from shore to shore as easily as we move the level of the coffee in our cups. He is the One whose voice says, “Let there be . . .” and there is. Let there be land. Let there be beasts. Let there be people. Let there be love and hope and sunshine and flowers and breath in our lungs. Let there be an opportunity that comes a thousand times a day to say that *He is God*. Let that sink in.

He is God. We are sheep in His pasture, and He cares for us with far more diligence and care than we deserve. When things look bleak, we can remember that *He is God*. Our perspective will shift as we dwell on the truth. God—*that* God—loves us as His own.

God,

You are holy. You are worthy to be praised. Thank You for allowing me the ability to be in Your presence and just sit with You. I pray as I commune with You that You would cover me with Your wisdom to stay focused on You and not lose sight of what needs to be done for the Kingdom. May You grant me the eyes to see spiritually and the heart to love others the way You have loved me.

In Jesus's name, Amen.

SOLITUDE

The Art of Solitude

"But when you pray, go into your room, close the door and pray to your Father, who is unseen. Then your Father, who sees what is done in secret, will reward you."

MATTHEW 6:6

She wanted to be a woman of integrity, and that had a lot more to do with her heart than her appearance. How would she handle herself when no one else was looking? When only God had a view to what made her tick and the choices she made? She wondered if people would look at her and see the overflow of her desire to be a woman after God's own heart. She prayed that it would be so.

Solitude isn't something that often drops in our laps. Even when we find ourselves alone, we might have a hard time enjoying it: we scroll, we worry, we busy ourselves with task lists. When was the last time you actually savored solitude? You set down your phone and turned off the television, told your loved ones what you were doing, and made space to be alone with God. You kept Him present in your mind and intentions. You told Him things that you hadn't told anyone else. You trusted Him with what was stirring in you and listened closely for His voice. Sometimes that kind of solitude feels daunting because we don't know what to say or don't think we have the time. We've lost the art of silence in someone's presence. But there's nothing God wants more. He longs for each of us to recognize that He is a safe place to land. Just read Psalm 91. As your hiding place and protection, God will be there for you. You can give Him everything without anyone else knowing, and you'll thrive because of it.

God,

thank You for always being there for me. With every tear shed, every cry, every silent battle I've had to go through, You were holding my hand, comforting me through some of the darkest moments of my life. Thank You for being a Father who sees me and goes before me. I cannot thank You enough for listening to my prayers publicly and privately.

In Jesus's name, Amen.

SOLITUDE

The Secret to Success

Tremble and do not sin;
when you are on your beds,
search your hearts and be silent.
PSALM 4:4

Why did she feel that she had something to prove? No one had told her so. God certainly hadn't. Still, she found herself striving to demonstrate her worth. The more she learned to trust what God said about her, though, the more comfortable she became in her own skin. Self-consciousness became confidence. Striving became surrender. And as she grew, she learned to tell others that they had nothing to prove. Just like her, they were loved and accepted too.

Ask ten people what they think it means to be successful, and you'll probably get ten different answers. Some might talk about money, and others might refer to inner fulfillment. One person might think success means having the job of their dreams, and another might think it's being a homeschool mom. Only God can define it, though. And our success has so much more to do with whether or not we're attempting to aim in His direction with every step we take. Only God can applaud or adjust our heart position for us. We don't know what we don't know, but we know He knows it all. So instead of trying to prove our worth, it makes so much more sense for us to let Him tell us of our value in His eyes. Are we loved by the Creator of the universe? Yes. Are we His children? Yes. Are we called by Him, chosen by Him, and forgiven when we surrender our hearts? Yes we are. There's no need to strive when God has given His stamp of approval on who we are.

God,
thank You for loving me just as I am and for leading me in loving You well. I know that my worth isn't defined by others, and that it's only through listening to You that I understand my role in the world. I need my time with You, when You can search my heart and direct my steps. Being Your child makes me a raging success!
In Jesus's name, Amen.

SOLITUDE

A Quiet Spirit

This is what the Sovereign Lord,
the Holy One of Israel, says:
"In repentance and rest is your salvation,
in quietness and trust is your strength."
ISAIAH 30:15

Even though her days were full in a good way, she still looked forward to the quietness before bedtime. In those moments she could let her spirit rest and reflect. She made a point of minimizing distractions before bedtime, enjoying the routine of winding down and letting her body direct the last several minutes of the day. When she really allowed the quietness in, she found herself stronger and surer. The quiet of night made her ready for the day.

A quiet spirit doesn't mean you have to be an introvert (although there's nothing wrong with that either). Having a quiet spirit doesn't mean you are invisible, unvaluable, or uninteresting. In fact, you could be the life of the party. You could be the one whom people expect good jokes from. You could be the parent who starts unplanned dance parties in the kitchen. You could run for president. A quiet spirit doesn't always belong to a quiet person. Quietness has more to do with the weightiness of our relationship with God. As we let Him in and allow Him to search our hearts, holding nothing back from Him and asking the Holy Spirit to do the work He wants to do, our spirits have no reason to be restless. When we settle into our identity in Christ, our inside places, which only God can see, are still and peaceful. How is your spirit today? Is there any part of you bucking against God's will? Is there any unsettled or anxious thought you need to hand over to Him? Learn to give Him all your parts, and your spirit will be so thankful.

God,

thank You for healing the parts of me that needed restoration. You have filled empty voids and comforted me many times. Thank You for always being there for me, for allowing me to rest in the midst of turmoil. You have been my Rock and my Strength. Your gentleness has brought me such peace, and I pray that when times get hard, I would remember how You came alongside me and helped heal my brokenness.

In Jesus's name, Amen.

SOLITUDE

Waiting for Thunder

Be still before the Lord, all mankind, because He has roused Himself from His holy dwelling.
ZECHARIAH 2:13

He was God, and she was not. And most days, she forgot that at some point. Most days, too, she wished at some point that she would keep Him closer and invite Him in more fully. Every time she found herself in an uncomfortable position, He was there to revive and restore her. Someday, she hoped, she would live with the knowledge of Him irreversibly and indelibly stamped in her line of sight. Letting God lead her was always the better way to go.

In a storm, when lightning cracks, our natural response is to pause and wait. Will the thunder come? We count the seconds between the flash and the reverberation to see how close it is to us. Why do we do that? Why does a loud sound impress us so much? Maybe it's less about the thunder and more about what it means. Something rare and potentially dangerous is in our midst. We get a sense that we're witnessing a display of God's power right here in our neighborhood. It will either cause a problem or roll on through, but it's impossible to ignore. I wonder what it would be like if the world saw God the way we see storms. What if we got a sense that He was near and ready to act, and we stopped everything and froze? What if we waited, holding our collective breath, knowing that His actions could cause great harm or great blessing? God deserves that kind of attention from us. We should be so in tune with His movements that we're constantly watching His moves. The more aware we are of God, the more confident we can be in life and in our choices.

God,

in these quiet moments I spend with You, I am reminded to surrender. I pray that as I surrender, You would release me from any doubts and fears that want to take me away from fully trusting in You. May I be still and listen to Your voice and not the noise around me. May I lean into You and rely completely on Your faithful promises.

In Jesus's name, Amen.

SOLITUDE

The heavens declare
the glory of God;
the skies proclaim
the work of His hands.

—PSALM 19:1

STEWARDSHIP

The Gift and the Challenge

It is required that those who have been given a trust must prove faithful.

I CORINTHIANS 4:2

Oh, she was blessed. She knew it. These children God had given her were precious and beautiful. They brought her joy and made her laugh, challenged her and invited her to grow exponentially as a parent and a person. It wasn't lost on her how important her role as a mother was. She was responsible for these amazing little humans as they grew and learned who God was. So she prayed constantly, asking God to help her carry the responsibility well.

Do you consider yourself wealthy? Maybe in the financial sense, but maybe also in ways that can't be measured quite so easily—family, friendships, a leadership role, a home of your own, a skill or gift that blesses others? What do you have that God gave you? We rarely recognize the gifts that God has given each of us. We take so much for granted. But along with the things that God entrusts us with comes the responsibility to steward those things well. Children are a great example. Many of us pray for children and recognize with joy that God has blessed us. But when they start talking back or make more messes than we can keep up with, we grumble and complain. But the messes come with the challenge of shepherding the children He has blessed us with. James 3:1 says that few people should want to be teachers of Scripture because of the responsibility that comes along with it. We can apply that to any gift, really—what God has given you, He hopes you'll use well.

God,

thank You for allowing me to play a significant part in furthering Your Kingdom and bringing glory to Your name. May I take care of the things in my life, whether big or small, that You have entrusted me with so I can be a testimony to those around me. You have blessed me. Therefore, I want to continue to remain faithful and true to who You have created me to be.

In Jesus's name, Amen.

STEWARDSHIP

What You Do with What You Have

"Whoever can be trusted with very little can also be trusted with much, and whoever is dishonest with very little will also be dishonest with much."

LUKE 16:10

The coworker who'd started after her had just been promoted, and it stung. Where were those who had seen how much effort she put into her own job? Why had she been passed over? Even as she ached, though, she remembered the truth. It wasn't about what she had so much as what she did with what she had. Her work fulfilled her. She appreciated her role. So she began doubling down on her efforts—not by working harder, but by working in a way that was fully devoted to God.

When others seem to receive what we think we deserve, it's hard not to feel jealous and even harder sometimes to celebrate with the ones who are celebrating. It often takes a few experiences for us to start realizing that circumstances are just object lessons for our life in Christ. He calls us to be humble, kind, and servant-hearted. He will give us many chances to practice. For example, how do you treat someone who cuts you off in line? How does your heart respond when a spouse mishears you or a child ignores you? Do you treat each person in your life the way Jesus would recommend? If you answer in ways you're not proud of, please don't feel bad. We're all on a journey, and God is so patient. Take what you have and make the most of it. In no time you'll find that God is giving more and more. He rewards those who are faithful to Him.

God,

help me to lead a life of service, a life dedicated to leading in a manner that is pleasing and honoring to You. May my life continue to be a witness to those who may not know You. May Your light continue to shine through me as I walk in obedience. May I steward this life that You have given me.

In Jesus's name, Amen.

STEWARDSHIP

The Fruit of the Spirit

" 'His master replied,
'Well done, good and faithful servant!
You have been faithful with a few things;
I will put you in charge of many things.
Come and share your master's happiness!' "

MATTHEW 25:21

It shocked her that much grew from her garden the year she really tried. It was tedious work, weeding and watering and fertilizing every day, without seeing results. Then the sprouts came, the leaves, the blossoms, and the fruit. As she plucked peppers, tomatoes, and beans that year, she felt the Holy Spirit remind her that her life with Christ was similar. Tend your garden, *she understood,* and much will come of it.

One of the most frustrating things about gardening is that it can't be rushed. In a world where we're ready for the next thing now, gardening happens on the garden's terms, not ours. There is no fast food where seeds are concerned. But that's exactly what makes spending time in the garden such a rich experience with God. On our knees, we work the soil and remove weeds. We tolerate some insects because they take care of others that would destroy the plants. We set up boundaries where bunnies or deer would eat our fruit. We watch diligently, feeling our hearts lighten at the first signs of success. When the harvest is meager or doesn't come, we wrestle with disappointment. But other times we have so much that we're sharing bushels with others and baking everything we can think of with the fruit from the garden. With God, it's the same. Our lives are the garden that the Holy Spirit works when we let Him, and nothing feels better than prospering in Christ.

God,

thank You for filling my lungs with Your breath. Thank You for ordering my steps and watching over me daily. May I remember that life is a gift and every moment is borrowed time. Help me to use the gifts You have given me to the best of my ability. I don't want to waste anything, but in everything, I want to remain faithful to the calling You have placed on my life.

In Jesus's name, Amen.

STEWARDSHIP

Our Gifts Make a Difference

Each of you should use whatever gift you have received to serve others, as faithful stewards of God's grace in its various forms.

I PETER 4:10

Sometimes she felt totally fulfilled in using her gifts for others. Nothing felt better than when she was serving well and knowing that God was pleased. Other times, she felt that she could do nothing right. Either her particular gifts were useless in the situation, or she was making mistakes and dropping the ball. No matter what, though, she knew it wasn't about her feelings. God had blessed her. She intended to serve in love at all times.

What makes your heart really sing? What lifts your spirits, fulfills you, and puts a smile on your face? Those might be the ways that you can be the hands and feet of Jesus to those around you. It might be in very practical ways, like helping those who need physical assistance, bringing meals to new parents, or providing for someone's financial needs. It might be in less-tangible ways, like listening with empathy, praying with someone, or offering encouragement to someone who's struggling. Your makeup is different from mine or anyone else's, and literally no one can fill your shoes. If one of us decides not to use our gifts, then it's like an orchestra with a missing instrument. If your church has a worship team, then maybe you've noticed the days when there's a drummer versus days when there's a *djembe* or no percussion at all. On days when there's no bass player, you might not immediately recognize what's different, but somehow *something* is missing. Each of us is meant to play a certain melody line in God's Kingdom, and He has given us what we need to play it well.

God,

thank You for Your gifts and for equipping me with the ability not only to serve others but also to share in Your love with them. Help me to steward my time well and use the gifts I've been given to lead others closer to You. May You receive all the honor and glory as You use me to further Your Kingdom.

In Jesus's name, Amen.

STEWARDSHIP

When the Master Plays

The earth is the Lord's, and everything in it, the world, and all who live in it.

PSALM 24:1

When she was inclined to give herself more credit than she should, she reminded herself of mountains. Not once had she moved one on her own, but she'd seen God do it over and over again. She remembered the destruction of a volcano—and then she thought of the incredible restoration and abundance that come as the land heals from such an eruption. God was God. She was not. Amen.

Thinking again of an orchestra, say that you are a violin. There's no situation in which a violin doesn't sound beautiful in the hands of one who knows how to play. As a violin, you may be used for joyous fiddling or somber laments. You may be taken to a subway platform to play for donations or into a specialized quartet for chamber music. You may join other violins of the same tone, making up an entire powerful section in a grand orchestra. Your Violinist, God, can work absolute wonders with you no matter where you are—as long as you are willing. The only thing that can keep Him from working is you. We all have the problem of ego, which rears its head when we forget the size of God compared to ourselves. At any moment, though, we can surrender again to His will. Then He can get back to work, sending the most beautiful strains of music through us and into the world. Everything belongs to Him, anyway. He's such a gentleman to let us decide to follow Him. And He's an absolute master to do with us what He is able.

God,
may You continually open my eyes to what You desire for me daily. I want to be aligned to every decision made by You, for everything that this world has belongs to You. May every opportunity glorify You and may my choices reflect the purpose that You have for my life. I want You to use me and my gifts for Your glory, Lord.
In Jesus's name, Amen.

STEWARDSHIP

Giving with God's Hand

Whatever you do, work at it with all your heart, as working for the Lord, not for human masters, since you know that you will receive an inheritance from the Lord as a reward. It is the Lord Christ you are serving.

COLOSSIANS 3:23–24

She could really have an attitude. Especially when she felt that someone wasn't taking her seriously or not listening fully to what she was saying. She strongly disliked being misunderstood, and unfortunately, she let that show. It was a process of practice and trusting God to learn how to enjoy working for Him and not for the world. As she learned to do it, she quickly discovered that working for God did great things for her own self too.

What keeps us from pouring out to others? Sometimes it's pure exhaustion. We run ourselves ragged for our families or workplaces, not listening to cues that we need rest. Soon there's simply nothing left to give because we're not giving God a chance to refill us. Sometimes we don't pour out to others because we want to keep everything we have. Due to poor upbringing or a mindset of never having enough, we cling to every last drop of God's generosity because we're afraid there won't be more. But we never, ever have to worry about that. The treasures of the Kingdom of God are endless. He is the most generous God. The more we share with others, the more He pours in—to overflowing, in fact—pressed down, shaken together, and running over (Luke 6:38). God loves our generosity in part because it allows Him to be generous right back. Plus, our willingness to serve others spreads the wealth. When we work for God, we are ambassadors for His generosity.

God,

I pray I always have a heart that is full of generosity. May I reflect Your grace and love for those who are in need. I want to serve the best way I know how. May You help me to steward my resources, time, and energy as I extend my hands. I want to always be open to what You are calling me to do, what You are truly wanting me to do.

In Jesus's name, Amen.

STEWARDSHIP

Without Pride

Be sure you know the condition of your flocks, give careful attention to your herds.

PROVERBS 27:23

Being brave wasn't her specialty, but she was learning. The world had screamed at her for years that she wasn't good enough and that she should stay quiet. As she built a relationship with God, though, she began to understand that she was meant to shine like a city on a hill. That didn't mean being brash and forceful, but bold in her love and ability. Submitted to God, she would only shine more brightly.

I once heard someone say that pride is a two-sided coin. On one side is the pride that puffs up. We talk ourselves up, cutting others down, making sure that everyone knows what we're capable of and how we think we should be treated. On the other side of the pride coin is the pride that pushes down. We tear ourselves apart in front of others, never receiving the acknowledgment of who God has made us to be, verbally berating our identity because we think that is a holy thing to do. But God was clear that pride of any sort goes against Him: He detests *all* the proud of heart (Proverbs 16:5). Pride is inward-focused and self-conscious. Our hearts are meant to be Holy Spirit–focused, and our minds are made for being God-conscious. As Paul said, our boasting should be in our weakness, not out of pride, but out of the knowledge of what God can and will do with it (II Corinthians 12:9). You, friend, are meant to shine confidently *because* you are weak. And He is strong. Own your beautiful place in His world—He made you for it.

God,

thank You for creating me with purpose. Forgive me if I ever downplay myself. You made me in Your image, as Your precious child. May I honor You by walking in my calling and not let fear hold me back. May I surrender my need to control everything and instead trust You in everything. May I continue to steward what I have been given.

In Jesus's name, Amen.

STEWARDSHIP

Prosperity, Really

"Bring the whole tithe into the storehouse, that there may be food in my house. Test me in this," says the Lord Almighty, "and see if I will not throw open the floodgates of heaven and pour out so much blessing that there will not be room enough to store it."

MALACHI 3:10

She loved her double mocha macchiato in the morning. Just saying it out loud made her mouth water. She'd had a growing sense lately that it had become a little too important. And though it was likely to kill her (not really), she decided to shift her focus. She set that precious money aside each day for a month, donating it at the end. It shocked her to see how much she'd saved in thirty days. She considered what the church or a charity could do with that money, and decided she'd be more careful with her spending from now on.

Does how you spend money feed into your sense of anxiety, or does it feed into your sense of peace? It's an important question to ask ourselves. Wealth has very little to do with the numbers we see when we check our account balances. It's more about the prosperity of our attitudes and spirits. This might sound very strange to you, but money might be one of those things that feeds into a healthy lifestyle. You might check your sleep, exercise, water intake, nutrition, and exposure to sunshine. But do you check your heart where money is concerned? Do you spend like you're owed a reward, or do you skimp out of fear? A balanced mindset toward money should give you a sense of calm inside, knowing that all things are made for our enjoyment and that buying something fun isn't wrong—but that it all belongs to God anyway, and He gives us what He hopes we'll steward well as we serve Him. A cheerful giver knows that money is actually made to prosper us from the *inside*.

God,

thank You for Your faithfulness. You continue to show up in all areas of my life, and You continue to reveal to me the things that truly matter to You. I pray as I continue to seek after You, the gifts that You have placed in me can be used wisely. I want to be a good steward of what You have blessed me with and not waste it on foolish things.

In Jesus's name, Amen.

STEWARDSHIP

The Serving That Serves the Servant

Each of you should give
what you have decided in your heart to give,
not reluctantly or under compulsion,
for God loves a cheerful giver.
II CORINTHIANS 9:7

It was a covert operation, and she loved being a part of it. With an open heart she went into public places, where she grocery-shopped or visited her kids' school. She waited expectantly for God to reveal a way to bless someone who needed it. And the opportunities came. It might be a twenty-dollar tip at the car wash. It might be paying for a small batch of items for the person behind her in line. They were rarely large transactions, but they took a large and special place in her heart.

God loves to work through us. He *loves* it. When we're constantly asking Him what He is up to, inviting Him to be powerful in and through us, then our own relationship with and awareness of Him grow.

It's for others that we work with Him, absolutely. But we can't help but benefit ourselves. We're like the river that flows with mountain runoff toward the sea. Along the river the trees and wildflowers thrive. Animals are fed and given drink. All because the river flows. It's the conduit from one place to another, but it is teeming with abundance. You and I will be conduits for God's good work, if only we ask Him. We will experience the well of living water springing up into eternal life (John 4:14). We will intend to bless others, but we will find ourselves incredibly blessed in the process. How can you allow God to work through you today?

God,

thank You for new opportunities to serve You. Show me how I can serve Your Kingdom today. Reveal to me people, places, and relationships where You desire for me to share my gifts. You have given me so much, and I desire to give back to You by loving on Your people. I want to honor You in all ways possible.

In Jesus's name, Amen.

STEWARDSHIP

Embracing the Present Moment

***He has made everything beautiful in its time.
He has also set eternity in the human heart;
yet no one can fathom what God
has done from beginning to end.***

ECCLESIASTES 3:11

She recognized that the world she lived in glorified the fast-paced life, rushing to the next thing, chasing after the next big dream. She knew she was guilty of falling into the trap of feeling as if she had to rush her way through life because she felt pressure to constantly achieve and succeed. It was easy to feel as if she were wasting the gifts God placed inside her if she was not constantly doing something.

When we start believing this lie, we can become overwhelmed with the heaviness of constantly being on the go. It is in these moments that we need to breathe, remember the importance of slowing down, turn to God, and then watch that guilt drift away. It is then that we can feel the peace of God and start taking time to embrace the ordinary. In Ecclesiastes 3:1, we are reminded that "there is a time for everything, and a season for every activity under the heavens." There is a time to hustle. But there is also a time to slow down, to savor life's simple pleasures, and to rest in God's presence. Doing that is taking good care of what God has given you. If you find yourself in a season when you feel like you are constantly rushing through life, why not pause for a moment? Take a few deep breaths and ask yourself why you feel pressured to hustle your way through the day. Talk to God about how your life seems to be moving too fast. Ask Him for refreshment. Ask Him to help you find time each day to slow down and appreciate the beauty of being in the moment. Ask Him to remove all the rushing, and to open your eyes to finding joy in the ordinary.

God,
may I continue to recognize Your presence in the simplicity of my everyday life. May I take the time to be mindful of every moment and see the extraordinary in the mundane. Every season serves a purpose; none is wasted.
In Jesus's name, Amen.

STEWARDSHIP

Breathe,
remember
the importance
of slowing down,
turn to God,
and then watch
that guilt
drift away.

—SOPHA RUSH

WONDER

True Excellence

Who among the gods is like you, Lord?
Who is like You—majestic in holiness,
awesome in glory, working wonders?
EXODUS 15:11

She looked up from her work and breathed. She'd been in her head a lot. But the sun was shining, and she could hear the sounds of happiness outside her window. Maybe she needed a break with the ones she loved most. Sure, she was busy. But nothing mattered more than truly living.

There's a big difference between perfection and excellence. When we seek perfection, we tend to get bogged down by overachievement and stress. We're aiming for not just a moving target, but a target that is far, far beyond our reach. We were never meant to be perfect or do perfect work. That is a job God wants to do Himself. Matthew 5:48 calls us to be perfect in the moment, which involves us living in the center of His will for our lives. Philippians 1:6 assures us that God will do the ongoing work in us so that one day we will be fully complete. But perfection as we usually see it—straight As or a household run with precision—just isn't what God desires. We wear ourselves out trying to act like God. Excellence, on the other hand, is taking the gifts He has given us and cultivating them. Excellence takes into account that God is the One who gives us any ability at all. We can give Him and the world the very best of what we've been given, continually growing, and that is a beautiful thing. What are the gifts that you use with excellence? Do you often consider being excellent in kindness, joy, and the other fruit of the Spirit? Consider where you put your efforts, and ask God if you're on track to gain excellence in His eyes.

God,
so often, my own interests and goals get in the way of the work You are doing in my life. I forget that You are so much greater, wiser, more eternal, and in control. May I stop regularly to remind myself of the difference in importance between You and me. Please keep me close to You so that I will always sense the size of You. Keep me humble.
In Jesus's name, Amen.

WONDER

Through a Mirror Dimly

Therefore, since we are receiving a kingdom that cannot be shaken, let us be thankful, and so worship God acceptably with reverence and awe.

HEBREWS 12:28

The world had tried to stop her. But every time she'd been beaten down, she had stood up again and kept going. She was bruised and scarred but stronger for it. She never stopped looking to Jesus as her lead. She prayed every day that her children would see resilience, determination, and shining hope when they looked at her. If they did, then all the scars were worth it.

Though the earth should move beneath your feet, God is unmovable. Though your circumstances want to defeat you, you are victorious in Christ. Though you wonder if you can possibly keep going for much longer, your wonderful Savior is beside you to lift you up and keep you on your feet. What you see today is only a glimmer of reality. I once frightened myself by walking past a mirror at nighttime. The dim movement over my shoulder, backlit by the night-light in the hall, made my heart skip. It was nothing! Just me in pajamas. But my mind and eyes knew there was *something* different going on. In Kingdom terms, we can only ever see dim glimpses of who we are in Christ. Our true strength and beauty will never fully be realized this side of heaven. I think that if we really knew the whole picture, we'd laugh at our troubles today. Especially things like losing our favorite pair of earrings or having to do the dishes. Remember today that what you see is temporary and unclear. Ask God for a view into His perspective, because He sees it all—and He is never shaken.

God,

the world around me shakes so easily. My family can be shaken by circumstances. I myself can quickly go into a funk if my plans don't pan out the way I hope. Teach me to surrender my expectations to You, trading them in for anticipation of all that You are capable of. May I constantly be amazed by who You are.

In Jesus's name, Amen.

WONDER

Transformation

Do not conform to the pattern of this world,
but be transformed by the renewing of your mind.
Then you will be able to test
and approve what God's will is—
His good, pleasing and perfect will.

ROMANS 12:2

She could tell that her thought patterns had changed. She remembered a time when fear would grip her daily, and she dealt with such anxiety over what she understood now to be minor concerns. But God had been working in her. Her stomach still fluttered at times. The worries still invited themselves in. But now she dismissed them and reminded herself of God's promises. She wasn't the same person she used to be.

When you begin to follow Jesus, you feel so much like the person you were just a moment before—but you are different. You might come tattooed and pierced, with questionable habits and unhealed hurts. Your mouth might run too much. Anger might control you. Your lifestyle might even go against Scripture. But none of this is God's immediate concern. Your heart belongs to Him now. He's not worried about the peripherals as long as you've come to Him. He can only work in you when you come to Him. From the moment you say yes to Him, the work begins. Your perspective begins to shift. Your interests change. Your heart softens. Your wounds heal. Over time you become a work in progress, showing beautiful movement toward radiance in Christ. And He can use absolutely anything. Tattooed and pierced, you may reach some who would be hesitant to talk to a perfectly pressed preacher. Your history might give you the ability to empathize with others who have similar pasts. God knows what He's doing, and His work never fails.

God,
thank You for creating humanity in such a way that we don't have to hustle to be loved. I am learning to allow Your work in me to change me from the inside out. Please show me how to surrender my own will so that I can fully understand Yours. May Your will be done in me.
In Jesus's name, Amen.

WONDER

Wonder-Filled

Let all the earth fear the Lord;
let all the people of the world revere Him.
PSALM 33:8

She saw God in the weeds. In a field of grass, those bright dots of color popped up all over, and it wasn't their fault that people had decided to name them something unflattering. Yellow dandelions, purple clover, star flowers, geraniums—they made an otherwise vast expanse of green look like a scene from a movie. It was too beautiful to be called an accident.

Where do you usually look for and find God's majesty? How do you purpose to cultivate wonder in your life? Is it in a baby's giggle? Is it in the sunrise or sunset? Do you find awe-inspiring beauty in the ocean or in beautiful acts of kindness? Stop for a few minutes today and really give that some thought. How do you, personally, live in wonder? As a rule, we don't spend much time marveling. Children do it so much more. A child will crouch in front of a leaf to watch a ladybug crawl. He'll practice and practice to see a rock skip across the lake. She'll tilt her head to the sky, looking for animals in the puffy clouds. As grown-ups we keep our gaze down as we plow forward, but we have a maturity that adds depth to marveling when we take the time for it: we see God in the way someone treats us or in the way someone we know unpretentiously serves another. We can sit for an hour by a creek side, listening to the sounds of a forest even as the tender voice of God speaks truth to our hearts. Living in wonder is simply recognizing that what we observe is beyond our human comprehension. May we never lose our sense of wonder.

God,

help me forever shift my perspective toward Your majesty and glory. I don't want to be so inwardly focused that I lose sight of You. May I genuinely fear You in holy ways; honoring You and holding those things sacred that You deem sacred. I pray that when others look at me, they see that my gaze is on You and my delight is in You.

In Jesus's name, Amen.

WONDER

Trust Fall

"But seek first His kingdom and His righteousness, and all these things will be given to you as well."
MATTHEW 6:33

She had learned to defend herself fiercely, and that was not what God wanted. She had learned to fight for her rights, and God was asking her to trust Him. He had not made her a weakling, ready to lie down and be trodden on. He had made her a meekling: *one with all the power of the Kingdom of God at her fingertips, but willing to step back and let Him defend her. Life with Him was exhilarating, challenging even—but so fun.*

"Whoever wants to save their life will lose it, but whoever loses their life for Me will find it" (Matthew 16:25). What a challenging message, especially for those of us who have grown up learning to rely most heavily on ourselves and our own abilities. Never mind those team-building "trust fall" exercises where your coworkers agree to catch you when you fall backward. For those of us who have had to learn how to stand alone and strong, surrender can feel as scary as leaning over the side of the Grand Canyon. When I struggle the hardest to lay aside the distraction of fixing things, I remember what Jesus lost in order to gain everything: "For the joy set before Him He endured the cross, scorning its shame, and sat down at the right hand of the throne of God" (Hebrews 12:2). Jesus could have fixed His problem. He had plenty to worry about. But He sought the Kingdom of God first and foremost, and we have everything to thank Him for now. What distractions are keeping you from the Kingdom today? Set your eyes right, trust Him, and take a step.

God,
people may say that being a Christian is boring, but I know that life with You is never boring. What an adventure! Allow me to live victoriously and joyously in Your presence, spending my life in awe of You and Your Kingdom. May I seek You above all and then watch as everything else slips into place. You are worth being amazed by.
In Jesus's name, Amen.

WONDER

How He Makes Us Feel

But for you who revere My name, the sun of righteousness will rise with healing in its rays. And you will go out and frolic like well-fed calves.

MALACHI 4:2

In a way, she was glad that vacations and special times didn't come all that often. Most of her life was fairly mundane on the surface. But when she found herself with toes in the sand or on a thrilling adventure, her soul lifted like a hot air balloon in a cloudless sky. She was reminded in those times that God was working on a glorious plan, and that one day she would feel even better than this one hundred percent of the time. She could hardly wait.

Do you know the feeling of looking forward to something? The "something" will be different for all of us, as well as the reasons we're excited about it. The next time you feel it, really ask yourself what you're looking forward to. It probably won't be the event itself, but the feeling that comes along with it. A favorite hike, for example, might be less about the particular place and more about the feeling of moving your body, fresh air on your skin, connection through conversation with someone you care about, and the awe-inspiring view at the end. Maybe you look forward to introducing your kids to roller skating—not because of the venue or the crowded floor, but because of the feeling you had as a child, breezing across the floor and feeling the vibrating roll under your toes. Maya Angelou once said that we will forget what people say, but we'll remember how they made us feel. How does God make you feel? What does spending time with Him do for your soul and spirit? As His children, these are the things we long for most.

God,
I have a feeling that I truly have no idea what the benefits are of following You. Something tells me that I'm only getting glimmers of all that it means to know You. Hone my instincts to draw close to You. Remind me with every breath that You are the Giver of good gifts and that You call me a daughter. Show me You love so that I never feel tempted to stray out of Your sight.
In Jesus's name, Amen.

WONDER

Knowing When

He must become greater;
I must become less.
JOHN 3:30

She loved the feeling of confidence that came when she knew what she was doing. She had come to realize wisdom was such a gift. Correctly discerning right from wrong was an art. And it had only been through the trial and error of living life with God that she had come this far. Even so, she knew her place with Him. She knew He was always *right, and she was only right by His grace. So she watched Him, every day, and followed His lead.*

If you've watched a nature documentary, you may have seen the members of a group of animals make way for their leader. A herd of elephants, for example, has a matriarch. She is at the front of the line when they walk somewhere. When she stops to rest or take a drink of water, the herd does the same. Each elephant is in charge of her own behavior, yet something internal guides her decision to let the matriarch guide the herd. When you and I are in tune with God, we have the internal compass of wisdom and discernment. The Holy Spirit leads us to make decisions that are mindful toward God and His Kingdom. We learn when to step forward boldly and when to rest under His wings. Anytime He displays His power in our lives, we learn to sit back in awe and let Him work. That happened with John the Baptist. He had loudly declared that the Messiah was coming, exhorting Jews to repent and be baptized. But when Jesus actually showed up, John was immediately silent. He knew it was time for the Leader, to lead. You and I are learning too. Know where God is in your life, what He's doing, and how you can best partner with Him for the Kingdom to come today.

God,

Just as John the Baptist knew when it was time to step back and let You take the spotlight, help me to know the right moments to completely let You lead and the right moments to step forward confidently in Your love. I invite the Holy Spirit to freely reign in my heart and mind, guiding my decisions and the way I view the world. May Your will be done in me always.

In Jesus's name, Amen.

WONDER

When You Need Him Most, and Always

Let us then approach God's throne of grace with confidence, so that we may receive mercy and find grace to help us in our time of need.

HEBREWS 4:16

Her heart was so tired of trying to be brave. She could feel the weightiness of something much too big for her. Finally, at the end of her rope, she looked up and tugged. Help! *A face appeared at the top end of the pit she was in: "It's about time, child," said God. He lifted her up and held her, already working to straighten out all that was crooked. He was that reliable and strong, and she was so glad.*

As children, our parents are the place we go when we need help. Parents can reach higher shelves. They can buy things we need. Their arms are longer for big hugs. If you had the experience of available parents, then you probably took their closeness for granted. If you had absent parents in any way, then you certainly felt the loss of having someone you could count on no matter what. We're meant to experience that feeling of having powerful people in our lives whom we can potentially take for granted. Because God is that parent for any of His children. In our times of need or joy, He is there. When we need comfort or guidance, God is that close. We can come to Him running as quickly as we used to when we'd fallen and skinned our knees. If you haven't had that before, I'm so sorry—but please know that you can have it now in Jesus. He is the King of the universe, but when you knock on the big, wide doors to His throne room, His face lights up. "Let her in," He says, as the doors swing wide. You are precious in His sight, and He loves you.

God,

may I never lose the wonder of having access to Your presence at the throne of grace. May I hold that privilege with great care and sacredness. You are the God of the universe, yet You see fit to love me personally. Help me to come to You often and with the right things. And teach me to demonstrate Your grace to those around me.

In Jesus's name, Amen.

WONDER

Facing the Rapids

"I have told you these things, so that in Me you may have peace. In this world you will have trouble. But take heart! I have overcome the world."

JOHN 16:33

She loved when all was right in her world. She subconsciously worked toward the happy medium where everything seemed in control. But she was also learning to appreciate the trials. Like a rafter approaching the rapids, she gripped the ropes more tightly and felt the flutter of her heart. She watched the guide who had done this a trillion times before with a trillion other people. Through the smooth and the choppy, she knew it would all be okay.

Trusting God with our emotions can feel impossible when we're in the thick of it. Everything in us screams to fix the problem and find comfort again. But what if we are meant to sit in discomfort sometimes? What if trials aren't something to be gotten rid of so much as they're opportunities to turn harder toward God and learn to trust Him more? After all, if we never had a chance of drowning, would we ever get to experience buoyancy? If we never knew hatred, would we ever learn the depth and intensity of God's love? If we never knew sorrow, would we ever appreciate joy or ever understand the beauty of authenticity and empathy? We might be better off to start seeing trials and troubles with expectant eyes. *What will God do this time? How will He get us through? What will we learn, and how will we become stronger?* As you consider your own array of circumstances today, thank Him in a new way for what your troubles will bring. Even if you don't know, He does!

God,

part of having faith like a child is accepting Your peace that passes understanding. I know that You are the One to run to in all things, and I want to live that way—for myself as well as anyone who looks my way. May I always have the eyes to see things the way You do, with love and anticipation of what You are going to do. I will take heart in You.

In Jesus's name, Amen.

WONDER

Learning to Dance

The fear of the Lord is the beginning of wisdom, and knowledge of the Holy One is understanding.
PROVERBS 9:10

The more she grew to know God, the more confident she became in His presence. The more she followed Jesus, the more in love with His heart she was. The more she communed with the Holy Spirit, the more she loved this life she had chosen. God was her everything. There was nothing to fear except losing Him—and she wasn't planning on that in her lifetime.

When you learn a new dance, you watch the choreographer closely. Your eyes never leave her feet or body as you drink in every movement. You watch the feeling she emotes by her facial expressions and the twists of her torso. As you begin to move, you do your best to emulate all you've observed. You keep watching, over and over again, until your body moves with the same precision and personality that the dance requires. And soon, others are watching you to see how it's done. So we are with God. Our Choreographer of life. There will never be a time when we know more or do better. Our eyes should be fixed on Him from now until eternity, when all will be beautiful. As we watch God intently, learning to reflect His movements and mind, others will see and learn from us. This is one way to think of the fear of the Lord. It doesn't mean mortal fear, per se. Not the kind that makes us cower in a corner (though He is definitely worthy of that). Fear of the Lord means to instinctively understand that He is the Source of all wisdom and knowledge. We pour every effort into never losing sight of Him. We learn to dance as He does, and we look more and more like Him as we do.

God,
when I think of the word **fear*****, it doesn't conjure up good feelings. Fear is negative when I entertain it in my heart toward anyone or anything but You. I know, though, that the fear of You is holy and healthy. It gives me the right perspective of my place with You, and it gives me confidence that You can and will care for me as only a good Father can. Teach me to fear You as You should be feared.***
In Jesus's name, Amen.

WONDER

Nobody ever
outgrows Scripture;
the book widens
and deepens
with our years.

—CHARLES SPURGEON

Dear Friend,

This book was prayerfully crafted with you, the reader, in mind. Every word, every sentence, every page was thoughtfully written, designed, and packaged to encourage you—right where you are this very moment. At DaySpring, our vision is to see every person experience the life-changing message of God's love. So, as we worked through rough drafts, design changes, edits, and details, we prayed for you to deeply experience His unfailing love, indescribable peace, and pure joy. It is our sincere hope that through these Truth-filled pages your heart will be blessed, knowing that God cares about you—your desires and disappointments, your challenges and dreams.

He knows. He cares. He loves you unconditionally.

BLESSINGS!
THE DAYSPRING BOOK TEAM